GARDEN ORNAMENT

By

GERTRUDE JEKYLL

ANTIQUE COLLECTORS' CLUB

First published by
Country Life/George Newnes Ltd. 1918
Reprinted 1982

Published for the Antique Collectors' Club
by the Antique Collectors' Club Ltd.

British Library CIP Data
Jekyll, Gertrude
  Garden ornament.
  1. Garden ornaments and furniture
  I. Title
  717   SB473.5
  ISBN 0 907462 16 2

Printed in England by Baron Publishing, Woodbridge, Suffolk

CONTENTS

INTRODUCTION

INTRODUCTION

IT is not till the time of Henry VIII. that we know of anything of importance in the way of ornamental gardening in England. Hitherto houses of any consideration had been castles, or in some measure places of defence, and their fortified precincts left but little room for anything but the barest utility. In earlier records there is mention in the 13th century of a garden made by Henry III. for the Queen at Woodstock, and an illuminated manuscript of the 15th century in the British Museum shows a small enclosed garden with a fountain and trellised hedge; but even this is not English. We only know that large orchards and vegetable gardens were attached to the religious houses, and that these must have been of great extent, when it is remembered that nearly one day in three was a day of enforced abstinence from flesh meat and that potatoes were unknown. A few flowers were grown in these gardens, but only for ceremonial decoration.

Vines were planted in Britain by the Romans in the earlier centuries of the Christian era, and their cultivation was continued throughout the middle ages, not always necessarily for wine but also for the making of vinegar or verjuice.

But by the middle of the 16th century, the country, after being for long in a condition of constant warfare and trouble, was at last in a state of security. Money was in abundance and great houses were built that need no longer be fortified. Whereas formerly their windows were restricted in size and might only look into an inner court, they could now be large and look abroad without any restraint, and the wholesome wish for a garden for pleasure and delight might be freely satisfied. For summer play a bowling green was made near the house, and "knotted" gardens of curious designs were filled with flowers. Fountains and other water delights flashed in the sun, and leafy "covert alleys" were planted for summer shade when passing from one portion of the garden to another. The great Palace of Nonsuch, built by Henry VIII., was embellished with every kind of external adornment, for the making of which a large number of Italian artists and workmen were brought over; for it was always chiefly from Italy that the example and inspiration of garden ornament was derived. It is much to be regretted that nothing of Nonsuch remains, for though there are still some fine examples of timber-framed houses of the better and manorial class, there is none of a palatial kind profusely decorated. For besides the large quantity of detached, sculptured ornament that is recorded, the external timbers of Nonsuch were covered with scales of slate, probably gilt, and the leading of the windows was also gilt.

Large orchards and gardens were planted at Hampton Court by Cardinal Wolsey, afterwards altered by the King. The details of these gardens are lost, though some of the original enclosures remain. But there are pictures showing the King's garden, with the beds bordered with wooden rails, and a number of slender posts carrying heraldic animals that hold small vanes; the rails and posts being painted in the Tudor colours of white and green.

A frequent feature in the older gardens was the "mount." It belonged to a time when the need for defence was not yet forgotten, for its purpose was to provide a raised place from which a view of the open country could be obtained. It took either of two forms; one of which was a detached mound or artificial hillock, either terraced with concentric paths and flights of steps or with one spiral path, and crowned with a building, either an open pavilion, or, in the more important places, a banqueting house. The other kind of mount was a bank of earth raised against some outer wall, or against the wall rising straight from the moat. In some places it is obvious that the bank was formed by the soil dug out to form that section of the moat.

But more extended ideas of gardening were to prevail in the days of Elizabeth, when a number of great houses were built, and such monuments as Longleat, Wollaton, Hardwick, Kirby and others remain to testify to the genius of the architects of the time and to the noble manner in which they grasped and made use of the new conditions and possibilities under which building might be carried on. It was not the great houses only that showed this advance, but the numberless manor houses that were then built, many of which happily remain to us as precious models of the most charming and sympathetic of human dwelling places. Many of these were surrounded by a moat, for the tradition of a need of some means of defence was hard to die; but we have also to remember that the garden and house would always need protection from deer and wolves, besides the lesser enemies, hares and rabbits.

In the case of the greater houses there was, on the entrance side, a walled forecourt; sometimes one forecourt after another, entered through important gateways. On the garden side, next the house, was a wide terrace, preferably some feet higher than the garden level, so that a good view was obtained of the flowery parterre below; or the flower garden might be enclosed also to right and left by other raised terraces, ending in a garden house or some kind of ornamental pavilion. A great flight of steps would descend from the terrace to the garden level. All these features, with their structural decoration of balustrade, moulded steps and ornamental buildings, were the work of the architect. It followed that the dominating lines of the building were protracted into the garden, and that the main forms, however much they might be subdivided, were always symmetrical and rectangular.

In some one of the divisions the maze or labyrinth was an exercise of ingenuity and a form of diversion that commended itself to the designers of Tudor and early Jacobean times and their employers. One can understand the attraction of a puzzling and time-wasting contrivance in the days when home-keeping for months on end, without a break, was the rule. In the present days of hurry and much changing of place, we need all the quiet and restful influences that our gardens can give, and the maze no longer comes within our desires.

Some of the details of the old Tudor gardens are to modern taste frivolous, and quite undesirable; such as the gilt birdcages and the swinging plates of coloured glass to flash in the sun, as described by Bacon. Then a great improvement on the panelled wooden rails or dwarf trellis round flower beds was the use of dwarf Box, so finely employed in Italy, and later to be adopted in France, Holland and England.

The more important garden ornaments, fountains, statues, vases and other works of sculpture, were not in general use in the gardens of the earlier Elizabethan houses; they were to come later, especially after the Restoration, when a great expansion of garden design took place. The magnificent gardens at Versailles had been laid out and built by the eminent garden architect Le Nôtre, some of whose designs were obtained for the additions and improvements carried out by Charles II. at Hampton Court in 1669. It was then that the great canal was made and the avenues of Limes were planted that are still in existence. The same influence pervaded all England, and in the larger number of the great places laid out at the end of the 17th century will be found the long lines of clearing in woodland or of special planting, diverging from one point, probably the middle of the main terrace. These lines give reposeful dignity and that impression of vast space that was aimed at by the leading designers of the French school. In the nearer portion of the wood (the "Bosquet" of the French, so familiar in the pictures of Boucher and his contemporaries), the trees were clipped to form walls of green; important points such as inner junctions of alleys, being punctuated by fountains or statues. These were the scenes of many brilliant summer fêtes in connexion with the near gardens, that were also walled with high hedges close-shorn, decorated with niches for sculpture and pierced with arches for the passage of the paths. But every style becomes liable to accretions that were not contemplated by its original founders and that are not always to its advantage; thus the French gardens of the 18th century were encumbered with a vast number of plants in pots placed along the terraces and garden paths, a fashion justly ridiculed by the critics of the day. But even through the reign of William and Mary, when it was inevitable that much Dutch influence would be likely to prevail, the large, simple schemes of the French style, and especially the long, converging woodland avenues and their lesser counterparts in the garden, still held their own. John Rose, gardener to Charles II. worked under the direct instruction of Le Nôtre. He was followed by the partners London and Wise, who in the reign of William and Mary made further large additions to the gardens of Hampton Court. These designers were succeeded by Switzer, Bridgeman, and Kent. With Kent, before the middle of the 18th century, came the change to the landscape style, when all straight lines became abhorrent and the old ways of gardening were considered barbarous and only worthy of abolition. Then, near the middle of the century came Lancelot Brown, who was widely employed and who continued to sweep away the older gardens with their parterres and trim hedges. Later in the century he was followed by Repton, and the same work went on.

Many writers of those days deplore the devastation of the old gardens that had existed for two hundred years, with their stores of sweet old flowers and medicinal herbs that were then rooted out and considered rubbish, in obedience to the fashion of the day. Now we justly prize the comparatively few of these old gardens that remain, whose owners, either too poor to employ the fashionable landscape gardener or too wise to allow the destruction of their cherished old-time possessions, kept them unharmed, to the great benefit of the generations to come.

It was not till early in the 19th century that the principle of the Italian garden was again recognised as desirable, and straight, wide terraces with noble stairways and flowery parterres were laid out by Sir Charles Barry and succeeding designers. By this time the possibilities of ornamental gardens were widened by the introduction of many kinds of tender exotic plants, and the desire to make use of these led to what we know as the bedding system. By the middle of the century this way of gardening was practised to the exclusion of almost all other horticultural consideration. The hardy plants of the older gardens were not thought worthy of cultivation and were banished, and even the smallest places must have their beds of tender plants put out for the summer months only. Happily a wholesome change again came about, and the last thirty years of the 19th century saw the old plants restored to favour, and their number largely increased by the discoveries of botanical travellers. The interest of modern gardens has also been greatly extended by the use of the flora of alpine regions of the world, and by the cultivation of the most beautiful of swamp and aquatic plants.

The latest development of garden progress has been brought about by architects having again, as in the beginning, made themselves responsible for the main lines, at least, of the garden, and by the designer, having now a knowledge of former styles, being able to look at the whole matter largely and see what form of garden may best suit a certain place and its environment. Each place is judged according to its own character and conditions, and upon a careful consideration of these so is the garden planned. Except in rare cases there is no need to keep rigidly to any one style; it is, in fact, almost impossible actually to define a style, for whether a garden is called Italian, French, Dutch or English, each one of these merges into and overlaps the other, for they all have features in common that vary only in detail or treatment.

But we have always to remember that it is to Italy that we have to look for examples of the highest development of ornamental features in connexion with garden design. When we remember the conditions under which the great gardens of Italy came into being, it is no longer a matter of wonder that they should stand out as examples of excellence, both in general design and in finished detail. For they were made at a time when there was that extraordinary revival of learning, and of development in all the branches of fine art that we know as the Italian Renaissance of the 15th and 16th centuries. And when we read of a giant in architecture such as Bramante, the creator of St. Peter's and the Vatican, designing, with Raffaelle, the gardens of the papal palace and those of other princely houses, and of all the most exalted talent that could be found being employed upon the gardens of the many palaces and pleasure houses of the courtly centres throughout the land; of the popes and princes of the great houses of Medici, Sforza, d'Este and the rest, giving their personal encouragement and pouring out their wealth for the making of their gardens, one is the better prepared for their splendid design and endless variety of sculptured ornament. Numbers of the best of these gardens have perished altogether, and of those that still exist many are in a state of ruin, but enough remain to impress us with the grandeur of style, and to delight us with admiration for the amazingly fertile invention and varied manner of treatment of the vast quantity of ornamental detail.

The way out from the villa to the garden usually conformed to the ancient Roman model of a pillared portico opening on to a wide terrace, commanding some beautiful view of enclosure or distance. On another face of the house there was a small private garden, closely contained within hedges of clipped box or ilex, and always a shady grove of ilex, cypress, bay and myrtle. The site of the villa was usually chosen on a mountain slope, or in such a place as would afford a bountiful supply of water by natural gravitation, in order to feed the many fountains, pools and rills whose sound and sight are both so precious in a southern climate. The greatest sculptors were the designers of the fountains, with their groups of Tritons, of the vases or urns that ornamented the piers of terrace and stairway, and of the many gods of the ancient mythology, whose statues, set in niches of clipped greenery, adorned the shady ways and other portions of the garden design. The hillside site necessitated much terracing and many important flights of steps, but a terrace near the house commonly led to some kind of pavilion of fine design where the princely host might entertain his friends, and receive the men of learning and science, the poets and others devoted to the fine arts, whom he delighted to honour.

It may also be considered that the ornamentation of gardens with architectural and sculptured detail would be the more insisted on because the resources of the time, compared with those of the present day, yielded so little of actual flower beauty. Roses they had of a few simple sorts, jasmine, violets, white lilies, honeysuckle and flag irises; of shrubs for garden use they had box and bay; juniper, ilex and cypress for clipped hedges. Of flowering shrubs such as we have in such profusion, we hear of none but orange and lemon, oleander, myrtle and perhaps pomegranate. Small wonder then, that with this restricted means of ornamentation by flowers there should be all the greater care that the garden should be made as beautiful as might be by the work of the sculptor and the architect.

It is hoped that these illustrations of all kinds of garden ornament, now brought together for convenient study and comparison, may serve, not only to quicken the interest in beautiful gardening but also to show how ornament may best be applied, according to the quality or calibre of any place. The descriptions and critical remarks are to be taken as suggestive rather than authoritative, but they will be useful in directing attention to the various objects and their judicious treatment, mainly as to the preservation of harmony and avoidance of incongruity. The overgrowth of good buildings by ivy and fast-growing climbing plants is pointed out in several instances; it is a matter that should receive much more attention, for ivy is answerable for the disintegration of much ancient masonry that ought to have been better guarded, and architecture of careful and refined character deserves better treatment than to be defaced or even obliterated by a rampant growth of common climbing plants.

ENTRANCE GATEWAYS

WOOD AND IRON GATES

ENTRANCE GATEWAYS

URING the time of the English Renaissance, beginning in the days of Henry VIII. and reaching its full development in the succeeding Tudor and Jacobean reigns, the most usual form of gateway piers, whether of brick or stone, was a structure of square section, finished with a cornice surmounted by a stone ball. In the more important examples, instead of a cornice only, there was often a whole entablature with a top ornament, which might be either a vase of lead or stone or some heraldic form or other sculptured figure. There were also architectural additions on either side, forming lesser gateways, or with niches only. The piers themselves often had niches in the lower portions, with sculptured ornament above, as in the flower-pot gates at Hampton Court. These niches were not necessarily for the placing of sculpture, but to gain the advantage of light and shade, an effect which is specially valuable where they occur in the flanking screens.

It was not till early in the 17th century that iron was used for any part of secular entrance gates in England, or indeed for any ornamental work connected with architecture other than ecclesiastical. In earlier times gates were of wood, strapped and bolted with iron, then of wooden framing with bars only of iron, and perhaps an iron cresting on the top. Gates of iron alone were only sparingly used in the time of Elizabeth and James I., and it was not till near the end of the 17th century that the finest examples of such gates were made in England, when that remarkable master in smith's work, Jean Tijou, was in England in the time of William and Mary. He left as memorials of his surprising genius the iron gates and screens at Hampton Court, and much other work either of his own, or produced under his immediate influence, at many of the great houses of the country. The fine drawing and wealth of detail, extremely rich and yet never over-crowded, distinguishes his work from all else in England. His designs are embellished with grotesque masks of a quality never equalled in iron, and his conventional treatment of natural form, as in the noble rendering of acanthus leaf, the simpler shapes of lily and tulip foliage, and the waved edge of bay, show not only his reverent admiration for these beautiful forms, but his exact perception of their right treatment in his material. Tijou was followed by Bakewell of Derby early in the 18th century, and a little later by the brothers Roberts, Welsh smiths of distinguished ability ; by Edney of Bristol about 1734, and by several noted smiths of London, among whom Robinson, a contemporary of Tijou, Partidge, Coalburn, Warren, and Buncker were those whose names are known as the producers of the best work of the 18th century. It did not necessarily follow that the great iron gates and screens had piers of brick or stone ; in many cases the pier was replaced by an iron pilaster, though the solidity of masonry has always a satisfying effect. Smaller examples throughout the land of equal merit remain to us of the work of these fine smiths in connexion with the entrances and gardens of manor houses and even of those of lesser consequence.

An early Tudor entrance archway at Acton Manor House, Gloucestershire.

Entrance archway at Keevil Manor, Wiltshire ; early 17th century.

Entrance gateway at Stibbington Hall, Huntingdonshire ; early 17th century.

Cold Ashton Manor House, near Bath. In this handsome doorway, of the early 17th century, which leads directly from the road to the main door, a portion of the upper part of the richly sculptured ornament, of Italian character, has been lost. The lowest step of the semi-circular flight is also wanting, or the roadway may have sunk from the original level.

Hampstead Marshall, near Newbury.   Details of sculptured ornament on panels of piers, of pure Renaissance design and treatment ; 17th century.

Renaissance gate piers of brick and stone at Hampstead Marshall ; late 17th century.

Stone gate piers with sculptured ornament at Hampstead Marshall.

Brick and stone gate piers at Hampstead Marshall with sculptured urns.

Piers with flanking gate-screens in an ornate Corinthian order with curved pediment, at Staunton Harold, Leicestershire, the seat of Earl Ferrers ; much resembling the entrance gateway of St. Mary's Church, Oxford.

Boringdon, Devon.   The stone balls so frequently used as a terminal ornament on gate
piers are here of so large a proportion that the other architectural details are unduly dwarfed.

Keevil Manor, Wilts.   The gateway appears to be of a rather later date than the Elizabethan house.

The 17th century gateway at Mapperton, Dorset.   The wooden gate with iron bars, though no doubt renewed, is of a very old type.

Wooden gate of excellent design at Cleeve Prior Manor, Worcestershire.

Wooden gate with iron bars, of early type, at Hutton-in-the-Forest, Cumberland.

Wooden gate at Eyam Hall, Derbyshire.

The "Flower-pot" gates at Hampton Court, designed by Wren and erected about 1699. They are of Portland Stone, surmounted by leaden figures of amorini bearing up baskets of fruit and flowers, by Jan Van Nost.

Early 18th century gate piers at Glynde, Sussex. Flint, with brick angles and wrought stone caps, with heraldic figures.

Groombridge Place, Kent; late 17th century. A good example of an early type of gate, with iron bars in a wooden framing and a cresting of spikes and fleurs-de-lys, such as preceded gates made all of iron. The handsome piers, which are inspired if not designed by Wren, have the accompanying niches set in an unusual position; they more commonly face the outer road. These fine piers ought to be kept clear of ivy.

Hampton Court, Middlesex. The Lion Gates. The towering gate piers are on a scale so large that they dwarf, and put entirely out of proportion, the iron gates that accompany them.

A pedimented archway of Renaissance design at Honington Hall, Warwickshire

An example of a beautiful gateway of brick and stone whose design is almost lost by the overgrowth of creepers; the whole is much obscured and the treatment of the junction of wall and arch is entirely obliterated.

An iron garden gate at the Villa Pamfili-Doria, close to Rome. Besides the more usual scrolls, the left-hand gate shows a suggestion of leaf form in open strap-work.

18th century iron garden gates at Penshurst, Kent, of excellent form and enrichment, by an unknown designer. The piers have much the same character as those by Wren at Chelsea Hospital.

Simple and dignified treatment of entrance to Notgrove Manor, Gloucestershire. The gate piers with
the slightly curved outer steps and the mounting block form a pleasantly harmonious combination.

Sydenham House. The entrance, looking across the two levels of the forecourt to this beautiful Devonshire house. The piers and ironwork, of excellent design, are probably of the late 17th century.

A quiet and dignified garden entrance through a high wall at Iford Manor, Wiltshire.

Entrance to Almshouses, Oundle, Northamptonshire. The obelisk ornament, which is here of unusual importance, was frequent in late Tudor and early Jacobean architecture.

Stone gateway with iron gate of rich Italian design at Balcaskie, Fifeshire. The treatment of enriched scroll and vertical bar is quite unusual. There is no sign of weakness such as might easily occur in a design of this character. Complete strength and satisfaction of eye is secured by the inner and outer bar in each leaf of the gate running up through the main open scrollwork.

Stone-capped piers and walls with a very simple but good iron gate. The piers and the bracket-shaped ramps leading down to the wall are in danger of overgrowth. Although the fine growth of the Tree Peonies is a credit to any garden, they are in this case placed too far forward towards the middle of the path. It would have been better for them to stand well back to right and left, so as to leave the bases of the piers visible and unencumbered.

Massive piers at Newton Ferrers, Cornwall.   The ball finials are over large in proportion.

Gateway at Tissington, Derbyshire, with moulded steps to outer road.
The iron gate is by Bakewell of Derby.

17th century stone-capped brick piers to a Tudor terrace wall, with moulded stone steps
to a water landing.

Gateway at Shobdon Court, Herefordshire, with wide pedimented stone piers.

Jacobean gate-piers with obelisk finials at Canons Ashby, Northamptonshire.

Wide pedimented gate-piers at Kirkleatham Hall, Yorkshire.   The
iron gates are plain, with a richly ornamented overthrow.

Kirby Hall, Northamptonshire.   Gateway with broken pediment and heraldic shields and
garlands.   A noble example of English Renaissance design and treatment.   Possibly the
work of Inigo Jones.

A garden gate at Wittersham House, Kent.

A modern garden gateway built with rays of red roofing tiles and local sandstone.

An unusual and delightful combination of entrance gateway and garden house at Poxwell
Manor, Dorsetshire.   A clever use of the same brick differently disposed is seen in the coping
of the thick wall.   The half-round pillars on each side of the gateway are carried up the full
height of the building and end in blunt, stone-capped finials.   It is to be regretted that ivy
should be allowed to obscure so much of this interesting work.

Breccles Hall, Norfolk. An interesting example of the use of brick, variously moulded. The wall-top is battlemented and rises to join the outer sides of the gateway by a series of crowsteps.

Breccles Hall, Norfolk. A notable example of the use of brick. The projecting piers and the considerable height above the crown of the arch give much dignity to this fine garden gateway.

Entrance from the road to a beautiful old house in the Sussex downland.

One of several garden gates at Inwood House, Somerset; the work of a London smith of the 18th century. It is worth noting that the very plain brick piers have no wrought stone cornices or capping of any kind. It is a case where a restrained growth of climbing plants— a little overdone on the left-hand pier, is allowable in order to cover this deficiency.

One of several fine iron gates at Harrowden Hall, Northamptonshire; possibly the work of Thomas Robinson, a noted London smith of the end of the 17th century. The stone gate-piers bear leaden figures of early Renaissance character.

A garden gate of elaborate Italian design at Hatfield House, Hertfordshire.

Entrance gates to Traquair House, Peeblesshire.   A good example of the treatment of iron
gates in the time of James II.

Entrance gateway to Anderson Manor, Dorsetshire. The treatment of this gate is that which became general after the time of James II., the gates opening under a strong fixed rail which serves to support a handsome scrollwork overthrow. There are also iron pilasters next the piers which are not only ornamental but keep the opening gate well away from the brickwork.

Iron gates at Notgrove Manor, Gloucestershire. This rather frequent arrangement of gate-piers, shallow steps and mounting block, with a straight path across a forecourt, has always an excellent effect. The strap and scroll ornament in the lower panels of the iron gate is confused by the inner leaves of the gate being folded back.

Beautiful iron gates at Aldermaston, Berks. They were removed from Midgeham House, for which place they were originally made for Lord Stawell by Warren of London.

Entrance gates at Temple Dinsley, Herts. The pilasters are finished with pyramidal finials and are connected with the railing by brackets serving as buttresses. The effect of the handsome overthrow is much enhanced by the horizontal panel on which it rests.

Harrowden Hall, Northamptonshire. Gate and screen between the wilderness and the enclosed garden, of simple but excellent design ; early 18th century. The pair of tall piers carry lead figures that are too small in proportion.

Chirk Castle, Denbighshire. These garden gates, with others of more importance in the same grounds, were the work of the celebrated smiths, the brothers Roberts, early in the 18th century.

Chatsworth, Derbyshire.   Stair gates by Richard Oddy, the gatesmith of Chatsworth.

Low gates to the bridge at Emral Hall, Flintshire. The work of the brothers Roberts early in the 18th century.

Garden hand gates at Inwood House, Somerset, of old Italian work. The figures of boys bearing platters of fruit and flowers are also imported.

Hand gate to the garden terrace at Norton Conyers, Yorks.   The simple form of the upright
bars of the gate gives all the more effect to the beautiful design of the pilasters and overthrow.
Said to be the work of Warren of London.

Hand gate to garden, Great Maytham, Kent. A charming arrangement of circular steps leading
to the iron gate. This has an unusual but effective arrangement of pilasters on a higher level
than the foot of the gate, so securing greater lateral space and width of view. Such good
ironwork ought not to be invaded by climbing plants.

Inigo Jones's Gateway at Chiswick House, Middlesex. It is to be hoped that this fine gateway will be kept clear from an overgrowth of ivy, such as has completely smothered the beautiful bridge in the grounds.

A charming hand gate in the garden at Tyninghame, Haddingtonshire. The circular-headed gate chiefly of open bars, but with a richly decorated lock-rail, opens within an iron arch filled with scrollwork, between two beautifully designed pilasters.

Gate from the Wilderness, Belton House, Grantham, by Thomas Robinson. The fine sense of design of the whole, the way the top rail of the paling swings up to a shoulder, bearing a graceful buttress bracket that leads to the rich pyramidal overthrow, is all delightfully satisfying.

A stone doorway with heavy oak door and postern.

Garden gateway at Chiswick House. The fine piers are cruelly overgrown with Ampelopsis.

Gate and stairway to the east entrance, Powis Castle, Montgomeryshire.

STEPS AND BALUSTRADES

STEPS AND BALUSTRADES

WHERE garden ground slopes steeply there will necessarily be terraces, near or far apart, according to the degree of the gradient, and they will be connected by flights of steps. The gardens of the Italian Renaissance, many of which were built on hillsides, give us the finest examples of such terraced treatment. In those of the great villas the retaining wall was crowned by a balustrade with piers at intervals, each pier bearing an urn or vase or sculptured figure. The stairs, in noble, easy flights, and the landings, were also bordered by a balustrade with piers bearing ornaments. Where the hillside falls rapidly and the space does not allow the steps to come in the natural and obvious way, namely at a right angle to the terrace, the difficulty leads to a simple device, which makes the stairway all the more beautiful and important. A landing is thrown forward on the upper level and the steps descend on either side in rectangular or circular form. In the older examples, the space of walling below the projecting landing, now in a recess enclosed by the double stairway, became the place for a wall fountain and basin with the best possible effect ; the whole then becomes the central object of the garden or wider terrace to which the stairs gave access.

Some such features were translated into English use in the gardens of the great houses built during the time that we know as the English Renaissance, and from that time onwards to examples of considerable magnificence in the case of those belonging to the later classical or Palladian buildings.

Stairways entirely of grass have been made with good effect ; the best being that at St. Catherine's Court, near Bath ; but it is always doubtful whether they are worth the long hours of careful labour that are needed for their frequent trimming and proper maintenance.

Double stairway at Chiswick House, a villa built by Lord Burlington.

Drayton House, Northamptonshire. Steps to the terrace on the east side.

St. Catherine's Court, near Bath. One of the most beautiful of old English gardens. The house, originally Tudor, with Jacobean additions, has the advantage of rising ground on the garden front. This is laid out in a succession of terraces connected by a number of flights of steps, with the very best effect.

A large simple garden stairway at Wootton Lodge, Staffordshire ; the plain treatment of step and parapet is in keeping with the severe dignity of the house. Some modern disproportion of the garden paths has led to an obvious error. It would be better for the path to come more forward so that only one step impinges on it.

Steps to Owlpen Manor, a beautiful old manor house in Gloucestershire. The moulded edge of the steps gives refinement and pleasant light and shade. The simple wooden railing is excellent; in perfect keeping with the reposeful character of the place.

Ven House, Somerset.   A noble stairway in three flights from terrace to garden.

St. Catherine's Court, near Bath.   The ever ascending garden stairway.

Harewood House, Yorkshire, designed by Carr of York. Garden balustrades and fountains were added later by Sir Charles Barry.

Stairway at the end of the Italian garden at Bowood, Wiltshire. So good a design, with ornaments so important, suggest the wish that the stairs might have been given greater width.

Stairway from terrace to garden at Brympton D'Evercy, Somerset. A good example though of a considerably later date than that of the house.

Steps to a wide landing, Hutton-in-the-Forest, Cumberland, beautifully framed and backed by large trees. The symmetry of the design is somewhat marred by the loss of the right-hand pier with sculptured panel, and the substitution of a round shaft and vase of another form.

Steps from the forecourt to the terrace, Eyam Hall, Derbyshire.   The steps and parapet are plainly built as befits the character of the simple, dignified house.

Steps at the Deanery Garden, Sonning, by Lutyens. The edges of the steps are not moulded, but light and shade is secured by the overhanging of the paving stones.

Circular steps from terrace at Newton Ferrers, Cornwall; early 18th century. The rude form of the balustrade denotes the use of granite.

Roughly moulded garden steps at Okeover Hall, Derbyshire.

One side of the garden stairway at Clifton Hall, Nottinghamshire. The design is a half hexagon in plan. The stairway is so rich in architectural design and sculpture that it seems remarkable that the steps should not have moulded edges.

Newton Ferrers, Cornwall. A noble flight of circular granite steps.

Entrance stairway at Wootton Lodge, Staffordshire. The very long flight of twenty-five steps is unusual in garden design ; it is customary to break the flight with a landing at not more than twelve to fifteen steps, but in this case the long, unbroken flight has an effect of dignity and simplicity that accords well with the severe character of the house.

A great garden stairway in three flights to Nashdom, Taplow, a modern house by Lutyens. The whole effect will be improved when the very high retaining wall is partly clothed with climbers. The plants themselves might with advantage have been more solid in character : Bay and Magnolia would have been preferable.

Wilton House, Salisbury.   Steps from the terrace next the house to the garden, said to have been designed by De Caux in the reign of Charles I.

Successive flights of steps in the garden at Tissington Hall, Derbyshire.   It is always a gain, as an opportunity for happy garden design, when ground slopes upwards away from the house and so gives an opportunity for some such arrangement of repeated terraces and flights of steps.

The riverside circular stairway at Clifton Hall, Nottingham.   Another stairway at Clifton of
nearly the same design, not circular but of three sides of an octagon, has an even better effect.

Stairway down from the garden at Harewood House, Yorkshire.   The stairway begins by a
landing brought out as a square projection, with two rectangular flights.   A succession of
circular bastions completes the fine effect of this noble retaining wall.

Straight and circular flights of steps plainly treated at Eyam Hall. Early Jacobean.

Melbourne, Derbyshire. A double flight of steps on the north side of the garden, with a landing between the flights, where a pathway on the middle level comes in through the yew hedge. The garden was designed by Henry Wise, in the French manner, in the earliest years of the 18th century.

Garden steps in the grounds of a group of two old houses at Northiam, Sussex, lately restored and connected.   The lower retaining wall, half round in plan, is broken at three points by stepped circles, whose inner circumference reverses the circle.   The design is agreeable from all points of view but is clearest from the raised terrace next to the house.

Steps at Stoneleigh Abbey, Warwickshire.   A weakness that sometimes shows in old work is noticeable on the right side of the lower flight, where a joint in the middle of the coping of the low parapet has sunk, leaving the upper face of the stonework hollow.   Another weakness, often to be observed in old lead work, is seen in the case of the fine pair of vases on the gate piers, which have settled much out of shape owing to the weight of the metal.

Hestercombe, Somerset. An important and interesting garden by Lutyens. The circular steps are repeated at the other angles of this section of the garden. The thick, overhanging flagstones give distinct light and shade.

A beautiful and thoughtful use of brick is shown, both in the concentric circular steps, and in the gate piers with their bold cornices at Packwood House, near Birmingham. Ivy such as is seen smothering the upper part of one of the piers should always be removed before it works irreparable injury.

The great green stairway at St. Catherine's Court.

Hewell Grange, Worcestershire. A place with much beautiful garden ornament. But the very long series of green terraces and steps, though curious and perhaps quite unique, has an effect of monotony from being overdone. The mind of the spectator is also disturbed by a consideration of the amount of summer labour that the good keeping of the grass steps and slopes must entail.

Steps from lawn to a lower level in a Dorsetshire garden. The good steps and their side walls deserve a more careful treatment of the accompanying bank, which is too steep and abrupt in relation to the stonework. It would be better if the foot of the bank came forward to the line of the second step from the bottom; and if the bank was clothed with some dwarf shrub, such as Cotoneaster, this would relieve and fill the unsatisfactory hollow space behind the piers.

A delightful narrow stairway at Court House, Painswick, widening into semi-
circular steps after passing the wall.   The fine stone and brickwork is too good
to be smothered with Ivy, which ought to be removed.

Garden steps at Eyam Hall; early 17th century. This good old house does not deserve the obliteration of the architecture of the doorway, wall face and window mullions by a common modern climbing plant.

St. Catherine's Court. One of the many beautiful scenes in this lovely garden.

Plain stone steps in steep woodland.

Stairway from close to river path, Tocknell's Court, Gloucestershire.   The
simple steps are in perfect keeping with what is near.

Almshouses at Stonyhurst College, designed by Sir Nicholas Shireburn.   The whole scene is impressive from its simple dignity.

Massive steps to an outer door.   The Ivy on the wall is here permissible, but
should not be allowed to encroach further.

Garden steps and pool at Drakestone, Gloucestershire, designed by
Major Oswald Milne.

Haddon Hall. The great flight of steps down from the terrace.

BALUSTRADES

Montacute, Somerset.   Wall and balustrade bounding the north-east side of the old forecourt—now a garden.   The wall is broken by a semi-circular bastion with an open pavilion formed by six columns with a roofing of three stone ribs carrying a crown of two intersecting circles.   Each pier dividing the panels of balustrading bears an obelisk.   At the outer angles are important garden houses.

Montacute. The same wall and balustrade from the great terrace on the upper level.

Balustrade and steps at Newton Ferrers, Cornwall.   The stonework, which is of granite, does not admit of other than simple treatment.

The Italian garden at Drayton House, Northamptonshire. The balustrade, with the balusters widely spaced, is purely Italian in character. The garden is rich in lead vases of fine design.

The great balustraded retaining wall at Balcaskie, Fifeshire.   The deep buttresses bearing classical sculptured busts form an unusual feature.

Uffington House, Stamford. The close-set balusters are of 18th century type.

Lead sphinx on a massive pedestal, forming a bold and effective ending to a balustrade at Compton Verney, Warwickshire.

Valencay, Indre, France.   Parapet wall built with circular openings ; the piers bearing handsome vases.

Parapet of retaining wall at the Villa Gamberaia, Florence.   The wall rises by ramps at intervals to a short length of higher level which carries a vase.

Easton Lodge, Essex. Italian feeling, delightfully adapted to a modern English garden by Mr. Harold Peto.

Balustrade of Italian character at Drayton House. Every alternate pier bears a lead vase of fine design and decoration.

Blickling Hall, Norfolk. The parapet of the bridge over the moat. The panels between the piers are not balustered, but are filled with a pierced ornament of circular form.

Balustrade and vases at Margam Park, Glamorganshire.

Balustrade at Cliveden, Bucks, with highly decorated piers bearing large orange-pots, and recessed seats. Brought from Italy.

Balustrade of Italian character at Cranborne Manor House, Dorset ; early 17th century.

Arcaded balustrade at Harlaxton Manor, Lincolnshire.

Cliveden, Bucks.   Italian balustrade with sculptured piers, water basins, and recessed seats, from the Villa Borghese, Rome.

Dyrham Park, Gloucestershire.   Balustrading to terrace and double flight of steps of good Italian character.

Stone balustrading surrounding a circular garden at Newbold Revel, Warwickshire.

Villa Lante, Viterbo. Parapet to pools, with large vases and obelisks, and other details of this richly ornamented garden of the Italian Renaissance.

Balustrade and seats at the Villa Lante, near Viterbo, Italy.

Montacute, Somerset.   Balustraded margin of a large fountain basin in the lower garden.
The graceful, wide-spaced balusters and general treatment recall that of some of the villas of
the Italian Renaissance at Frascati.

Parapet to moat, built with quarter-round tiles, at Loseley, Surrey.

URNS, VASES AND
SCULPTURED ORNAMENTS

URNS, VASES AND SCULPTURED ORNAMENT

THE use of such garden ornamentation came to us from Italy; in fact, many of the examples were actually imported. Wealthy and illustrious English travellers could hardly fail to desire some reproduction of the splendid gardens of the villas they had seen, or where in some cases they had been entertained. Their admiration scarcely made enough allowance for the difference of climate, for one can hardly fail to observe that when some kinds of purely Italian ornament are introduced, that the effect remains exotic and cannot be fitly acclimatized. The busts of the Cæsars and other ornaments and sculptures in white marble are not quite at home in our gardens, and we only gain the true Italian feeling in the case of such places as Balcarres and Brockenhurst, where it is due to the personal genius of the designer and the admirable manner in which he has insisted on the complete and right rendering of every item of the project. Then in Italy, the marble vase may keep its growing aloe or myrtle, whereas in England for half the year the vase is empty. In fact, white marble is not a stone for English outdoor use—we have more suitable material in our home quarries. It is true that the greater number of our native stones encrust too readily from weather and lichen to be quite suitable for delicate sculpture, though in the case of balustrades and urns, seats and bases of sundials this is of less account. The question remains whether any fine sculpture of figure subjects, other than those ornamentally treated, such as *puttini* bearing baskets of fruit and flowers, or figures of rugged aspect, such as the Tritons of water fountains, are suitable for England unless they are under cover? There can scarcely be a doubt that the happiest material for our garden sculpture and ornament is lead, and many are the examples in this material of highly successful treatment of figure subjects, both from models of antiquity and from those of later origin. But it is especially in urns and vases that our lead-work excels, as in the splendid examples at Melbourne, Drayton, and Hampton Court; moreover, the surface of the metal, with age and exposure, acquires a delightful *patina* of silvery grey that harmonizes well with our garden evergreens.

Richly ornamented Urn on the Orangery Terrace at Margam Park,
Glamorganshire.

Pier and finial at Gayhurst, Buckinghamshire. One of several that occur at intervals in a wall of clipped evergreen.

The Emperors' Walk at Grimston, Yorkshire.   The gardens, the work of Nesfield, are of Italian feeling throughout and have numerous Italian sculptures, both ancient and modern.   It may be questioned, whether in our climate it would not have been better to dispose the pillared busts of the twelve Cæsars within some kind of shelter, or at least in niches of greenery.

Villa Albani, Rome, with sculpture in niches in the cypress hedge.

The sunk garden at Longford Castle, Wiltshire.   Near the end of this long garden of formal design stands the temple, and here the boundaries of the parterre draw in by a half circle to the great flight of steps which again leads to a long vista beyond.

Classical busts on short columns at Madresfield Court. The niches are barely high enough to be in good proportion to the sculpture.

Villa Pamfili-Doria. Rome.   The garden of this noble palace is rich in these giant terra-cotta
pots with their ancient orange trees.

French vases of stone at Wrest Park, Bedfordshire.

A group of lead sculpture at Wrest Park.

Lead figures of Roman warriors in the garden at Treworgey, Cornwall. The figures, standing detached from any architectural feature, are not very happily placed. Their proper place would be on the main piers of a balustrade or some other salient point of definite design.

Classical gateway and pillared screen at Easton Neston, Northamptonshire.   18th century.

Steps and basins, terminal figures, and other sculptured ornament at the Villa Albani, Rome.

Stone vases at Melton Constable, Norfolk.

Italian oil jars on the South Terrace at Hill Hall, Essex.

Italian well-head in the form of a capital at Kingston Lacy, Dorset.

Italian well-head in the rose garden at Plaish Hall, Shropshire.

Lead sphinx at Buckland, Berkshire.

Lead sphinx at Chiswick House.

Groups of cupids bearing up baskets of fruit and flowers at Vaux le Vicomte.   Graceful examples
of garden sculpture in the French-Italian manner.

Heveningham Hall, Suffolk.   Architectural screen returning forward from the end of the
house, with niche for statue, forming a stop to the end of the terrace with excellent effect.
The niche would bear a statue of larger proportion.

Trophy of fruit on an enriched square baluster base at Castle Howard.

A highly decorated marble vase on a plinth of classical altar form at Dogmersfield Park, Hampshire.

Lead vase at Brantingham Thorpe, Yorkshire.

Vase with Bacchic emblems at Panshanger.

Stone and bronze. A terminal figure of Pan piping to dancing figures of a young faun and a young satyr. One of the most successful groups of modern sculptured garden ornament. By Lady Feodora Gleichen.

Lead figures, probably of foreign make, in the gardens of Inwood House, Somerset.

18th century coloured lead figures at Tyninghame, Haddingtonshire.

Italian sculpture in the garden at Balcaskie, Fifeshire.   The " spinario " in the foreground.

A very fine lead cistern at St. Fagan's, Cardiff.   It has two ranges of rectangular panels filled
with architectural and heraldic ornament and a richly decorated frieze.   It stands about four
feet high and is dated 1620.

Group in lead, the Rape of the Sabines, by John
of Bologna, at Pains Hill, Surrey.

A highly decorated lead vase at Pains Hill,
probably by Jan Van Nost.

Lead figure from antique model at Rousham, Oxfordshire.

Harrowden Hall, Northamptonshire. Lead group of Samson slaying
a Philistine, often called "Cain and Abel"; the original by John of
Bologna.

Lead figure of kneeling slave at Melbourne, Derbyshire. The slave is an Asiatic; the more usual form is a blackamoor.

Lead statue of Actæon at Faulkbourne Hall, Essex.

Bronze vases at Nether Swell Manor, Gloucestershire.   Modelled by Claude Ballin, goldsmith
to Louis XIV.   Some of them came from Bagatelle.

Lead boys at Wilton House.

Lead vase at Hampton Court.

Lead statue of the Duke of Marlborough
formerly at Glemham Hall, Suffolk.

Lead figure of a cymbal player, from the
antique, at Rousham, Oxfordshire.

The piping shepherd and his dog at Powis Castle. One
of the lead figures on the piers of the balustrade to the
third terrace.

Lead statue of Mercury at Holme Lacy; the original by John of Bologna.
This statue formerly stood on the centre of the pediment of the main front of
Holme Lacy; in its present position it badly needs some kind of base.

Italian flower vase with tulips at Condover Hall.

Terminal figures bearing vases at the Villa Farnese.

Powis Castle. The lead figures on the balustrade of the third terrace.

STONE-PAVED COURTS, PAVED WAYS AND GARDEN SEATS

STONE-PAVED COURTS, PAVED WAYS AND GARDEN SEATS

IF one may assume a typical arrangement of the entrance front of one of the fine old manor houses of the 16th and 17th centuries, one may say that it stood anything from forty to seventy feet back from the road, with an enclosed forecourt either all paved or with flagged path with grass on each side ; the path passing straight from the road to the front door. If the house stood on a slightly higher level there would be a few steps flanked on either side by a dwarf retaining wall at some point on the approach a good deal nearer the house than the front entrance, and this upper space would be entirely paved. In many cases these manor house entrances have more recently been made into gardens, and one cannot but think that the gardening has often been overdone ; for it is the safest rule to keep the entrance side quiet as to showy flowers, and to reserve the main display for the garden front of the house. Such a rule always works out well in practice, and indeed the use of such restraint involves no penance, for what is more delightful than Box, Bay, and Rosemary, Skimmia and Alpenrose, and the handsome ground greenery of Lent Hellebore, Megasea, and Acanthus ? A large proportion of these green things with a few flowers only, such as Lilies, China Rose and Columbines, gives an appearance of dignity to an entrance court such as would only be lessened by a more lavish use of flowers.

It is a different matter in the case of a paved place which is purely a garden court, that is, an enclosed space of actual flower garden ; for here the bright flowers are strictly in place.

In the matter of paving, as in all others pertaining to garden design and ornament, we look to Italy for the finest prototypes. The illustrations of different views in an open court of the Vatican gardens show a use of stone paving in large, simple forms, such as is dignified in itself and in no way competes with the magnificence of the adjoining structures. It may well be carefully studied as a desirable method of treatment.

The beautiful garden seats of some of the Italian villas have also never been surpassed, and though stone seats are scarcely suited to our climate, yet, when the garden design has to conform to the style of a palatial building, the use of stone can hardly be avoided. At least they are good for the eye to repose upon, when they have a backing of yew or box and a further background of large trees with their ample shade. For gardens of lesser pretension we may have wooden seats, either of hard wood or painted. The common habit of painting garden seats a dead white is certainly open to criticism. The seat should not be made too conspicuous. Like all other painted things about a garden : gates, railings, or flower-tubs, the painting should be such as to suit the environment ; it should in no case be so glaring as to draw almost exclusive attention to itself. Such a defect is clearly noticeable in some of the illustrations. There is a convention among painters that flower-tubs should be painted a crude green and the iron hoops black, and that gates should be painted dead white and the hinges and latches dead black. It would be better if the seats and gates, ironwork and all, were painted either a grey like the colour of old weather-boarding or some very quiet tone of green, and the tubs any tint of green that is less green than the leaves of the plants they contain.

The paved court of the Villa Medici in the Vatican Garden, Rome.

Paved court in the garden of the Vatican. The pavement, of large and simple design, is an admirable groundwork to the highly decorated façade of the Villa Medici.

Paved court forming a rose garden at Waterston Manor Dorsetshire.

A garden court on the south-west side at Heale House, Wiltshire. Well laid out with a broad flagged terrace. The figures of gladiators on the piers of the balustrade are of bronze.

Paved terrace at the entrance to Kildwick Hall, Yorkshire.

Garden forecourt of an artist's home at West Burton, Sussex, in the midst of pastoral and downland scenery.

The wide flagged garden terrace at Iford Manor, Wiltshire, bordered by shrubs in tubs and other ornaments.

The flagged path across the quiet garden.

Flagged court at the Deanery Garden, Sonning.

The paved rose garden at Orchards ; a typical West Surrey house by Lutyens.

The paved court of the Villa Medici in the Vatican Gardens. A notable example of bold and simple treatment in two kinds of stone in large forms.

Pavement planting rather overdone.

Paved paths and platform in the sunk garden at Ewhurst, Hampshire.

Paved terrace and gateway at Mounton House, Chepstow, by Mr. Avray Tipping.

Shrubbery paths paved with stone setts.   It is doubtful, in a place where the lines of paths are free and informal, whether it is desirable to use a material which makes the outline of the path hard and distinct and the whole path unduly conspicuous.

Paved terrace at Fountain's Hall, Yorkshire.   The overgrowth of Ampelopsis on this fine house is much to be regretted.

A paved garden at Brinsop Court, Hereford. The ancient buildings are well suited by the pleasant planting of Roses, Rosemary, etc.

A paved garden court to a modern house, Lennoxwood, Windlesham, by the late Charles Mallows.

Angle of paved court with loggia at Burford Priory, Oxfordshire.   Early Jacobean work of
Renaissance character.

Flagged terrace at Hall-i'-th'-wood, Lancashire.

Wide paved alleys in the garden at Rous Lench Court, Worcestershire.

Goddards, Abinger Common, Surrey. The platform in the foreground combines a centre of a disused millstone with a filling of brick and a border of flagstone.

GARDEN SEATS

A stone terrace seat at Hackwood Park, Hampshire, flanked by vases on moulded plinths.

Modern stone seat at Hinton Admiral, Hampshire, of good Italian design. The segmental seat has sculptured ends and piers bearing *amorini*. The whole design is appreciably dignified by the bold projection of the pavement.

A modern oak seat by Lutyens, at Buckhurst Park, Essex.

Stone seat at Danby Hall, Yorks, of good Italian character. Its effect will be much improved when the screen of evergreen at the back has grown as solid and perfect as the arched hedge that returns forward.

A painted wooden seat at The Moot, Wiltshire. This seat, of an ingenious design of far-eastern character, would be better if painted less obtrusively. As very frequently happens, a seat painted white, or some very light colour, attracts overmuch attention to itself, to the detriment of other near interests.

Segmental seat at Sedgwick, Sussex.

Stone seat on the Bowling Green at Gravetye Manor, Sussex.

Wooden seats of a good simple pattern at Drakelowe, Derbyshire.

Curved stone seat with sculptured ends and central vase. Stone table in front.

Garden Temple with seat at Holkham, Norfolk. This is an example of a building on which no creeping plants should be allowed.

Good plain wooden seats at Haddon Hall.

A wooden garden
seat adapted from
an 18th century
design.

Painted seats in an
out-door parlour
at Wittersham
House, Kent.

Oak seat in a re-
cessed wall with a
tiled roof over,
at Westbrook,
Surrey.

LOGGIAS

LOGGIAS

IN the great houses of the English Renaissance the most frequent treatment of the main terrace on the garden front was that it was stopped at the two ends by a wall or balustrade, and that a flight of steps in the middle of the length descended to the garden level ; the steps being in immediate connection with an entrance to the house. There is a beautiful example at Cranborne Manor where an open, pillared porch, recalling the loggias of Italy, forms a delightful outdoor sitting room. At Bramshill there is another such place. The terrace, here forming a narrow bowling green between paved paths, is stopped by a projecting wing of the house, treated as a loggia on the terrace level. In recent years we have profited by such examples and have widened their scope of usefulness, for architects are now often desired to plan open air dining rooms for summer use, resulting in many ingenious adaptations of the loggia. The example shown at Rotherfield Hall, where an angle of the building on the bedroom floor is formed into a roomy open space, recalls the summer comfort of the better class of houses built on the Swiss Châlet plan, where such open air adjuncts to bedrooms are of untold value to all, and especially to invalids.

The loggia feeling of Italy was also strongly expressed in the great covered bridges of classical design, built under the influence of Inigo Jones, such as those at Wilton and Stowe ; for not only are they examples of palatial ornament in the landscape, but they are all the more impressive when seen close at hand, from their dignified architectural expression and their admirable connection with the near lines of the garden design.

Among the most successful of the modern open air rooms are the beautiful examples by Mr. Harold Peto in the houses recently built to his design on the Riviera.

The loggia at Cranborne Manor House, Dorsetshire; early Jacobean; about 1612.

The loggia, Cranborne Manor House, Dorsetshire. Interior.

Steps to terrace and loggia at Cranborne Manor House, Dorsetshire.

Loggia at Dingley Hall, Northamptonshire.

Interior of loggia at Bramshill Park, Hampshire.

The bowling-green terrace and loggia at Bramshill Park, Hampshire.

The loggia at Holland House, Kensington ; early 17th century.

The south porch at Cranborne Manor House, Dorsetshire.

Porch or loggia at Iford Manor, Wilts.   It may be suggested that the scale is too small for the
right use of Ionic columns.

Wilton House, Salisbury.   A long garden vista from within the Palladian bridge.
It is believed that the bridge was the work of a pupil of Inigo Jones.

A loggia on the bedroom floor at Rotherfield Hall, Sussex.

Loggia below and wide balcony above at The Villa Sylvia, Alpes Maritimes ; by Mr. Harold
Peto.   The architecture is in danger of undue overgrowth.

Loggia of the Lions in the gardens of the Villa Borghese, Rome.

The Palladian bridge at Stowe House, Buckinghamshire ; middle 18th century.

The loggia at Maryland, Alpes Maritimes. By Mr. Harold Peto.

Wren's colonnade on the south side of the Clock Court at Hampton Court Palace. Built in
the reign of William and Mary about the year 1691.

ORANGERIES

ORANGERIES

THE orangery became a necessary adjunct to the great house when the fashion was adopted from France and Italy of having orange and other tender trees in tubs for the summer ornament of the great terrace. Orangeries such as were built at Bowood, Longleat and Belton were structures of considerable magnificence. Columns supporting a whole entablature, surmounted by a decorated pediment would adorn the entrance, and there would be a central domed pavilion or some such building at either end. The roof was veiled by a handsome balustrade, whose piers, corresponding with the pilasters below, carried urns or statuary. In the case of those built under the influence of Wren, such as the one at Belton, where the very large glazed panels divided by a slender pier or pilaster might give a sense of weakness, this was corrected by the end panels being made much narrower, with a solid parapet above in place of the open balustrade. At Wrest, the fine orangery has had the usual low-pitched roof of slate replaced with glass.

Bowood, Wiltshire. The orangery, an imposing building, stands on the north side of the upper level of the large Italian garden, both sheltering the garden and acting as a screen to the stables. The house, and presumably the orangery, is the work of the brothers Adam.

The Orangery, Longleat, Wilts; end of 17th or early 18th century.

Classical orangery at Croome Court, Worcestershire.

A modern orangery by Sir Edwin Lutyens, at Hestercombe, Somerset.

Orangery at Eydon Hall, Northamptonshire.   The structure has roof lights which are unknown
in earlier examples.

Orangery at Apethorpe Hall, Northamptonshire.   The close parapet, completely concealing
the roof gives an opportunity for the substitution of a glass roof, to the great advantage of the
plants housed.

Orangery at Cassiobury, Hertfordshire, with panels of treillage between the lights and a roof parapet also of treillage.

The great orangery at Belton House, Lincs., of fine architectural design. The parapet is balustraded except at the angles and returns, and the piers are ornamented with sculptured figures.

A glazed passage-way as conservatory at The Pleasance, Gullane.

A new conservatory added to an old house. By Mr. Avray Tipping. The glass
roof is pleasantly concealed by the panelled parapet. It forms a passage way connecting
two parts of a building, such as might often be contrived in other places with good effect.

Orangery at Wrest Park, Bedfordshire. In the case of this handsome building, the glass lights, which have been substituted for the original roof, are nearly hidden by the balustraded parapet.

Orangery at Heveningham Hall, Suffolk. A bowed glass roof has been substituted for the original roofing. The cast-iron cresting to the ridge and hips of the new roof is a doubtful advantage, calling undue attention to what is, architecturally, of the nature of a blemish.

One of the most important and beautifully designed Orangeries is at Stowe, the great 17th century palace of the Temples in Buckinghamshire, now the seat of the Master of Kinloss. Everything at Stowe is on a large scale and is treated in the grand manner. The immense flight of steps on the garden front, and the Corinthian portico with its doorway flanked by niches holding sculpture, and its frieze sculptured with figure subjects in high relief, with the connecting pillared galleries leading to large outer pavilions; its entrance portico of the same character flanked by colonnades connecting the main block with outer buildings—all convey the impression of architectural magnificence. The curved range of orangery, with its central domed pavilion and pedimented ends, is in keeping with the rest. The ceiling of the dome is decorated with a painted vine trellis and with classical figures bearing garlands.

The Orangery at Stowe, Buckinghamshire.

The Ceiling of the Dome.

The Approach to the Pavilion.

GARDEN HOUSES AND DOVECOTES

GARDEN HOUSES AND DOVECOTES

IT was usual for the garden of the great house to have some kind of detached buildings, frequently at the angles of walls, where they might serve as retired places for study or repose, or, in the case of the larger examples, as summer banqueting houses. They were also placed at the ends of raised terraces, commanding a view of the enclosed garden or parterre on the one hand and of the park or open country on the other. Since the Tudor days, when the sumptuous garden houses at Montacute were built, the comfort of having such places of refuge has always been felt, and the illustrations show the many ways in which the need has been fulfilled, for the varied buildings range from the classical temple of the 18th century to the humble summerhouse of the modest garden. Some of the temples and pavilions of Palladian design were intended for pure ornament, to complete and conclude a garden or woodland vista, but for the most part they had suitable seats, or sheltered spaces that would allow of the placing of seats and tables. Many were wholly enclosed and had a fireplace and windows. Comfortable lighting is often forgotten when summerhouses are built, but it is just the provision of proper light that makes them available for reading or any such purpose. If it is not attended to the use of the place is wastefully restricted. Often an open summerhouse has the light from the entrance only ; there should always be a side light ; if it is an enclosed building and there is a fireplace, the light should be on the left side as the sitter faces the fire. The better design of garden houses has of late been carefully considered by architects, especially now that many people desire to have a dining room partly in the open air.

In the old days when pigeons were depended on as a source of food, and large flocks were kept, the pigeon house took its place in the garden design. Some of these, either circular or rectangular in plan, occur at the angles of garden walls, but others are quite detached and are buildings of some importance. There are also to be occasionally seen in old gardens interesting shelters for bee-hives, usually structures of wood, straw-thatched, though one example shown is of solid masonry.

18th century hexagonal garden temple of classical design with domed roof, at The Moot, Wiltshire.

Lyddington Bede House, Rutland. An ancient, tower-like building at the angle of two walls. The pathway passes through the lower story. Access to the upper is on the higher level at the back of the wall.

Entrance front of a garden house at Stonyhurst College, Lancashire.

Terrace with side view of a garden house at Stonyhurst College, Lancashire.

Garden house at Murthly Castle, Perthshire ; with additions, adapting it to serve as a cottage.

Montacute, Somerset. One of the two garden houses at the angle of the terrace wall. This one stands on the south-east side of the garden that was formerly the entrance forecourt.

Domed temple in the gardens of Duncombe Park, Yorkshire.   The rolls of the lead roofing are accentuated to form a decorative feature.

Garden temple with domed roof and pillared portico at Chiswick House, Middlesex.

Ionic temple with domed roof and enriched frieze at Hall Barn, Buckinghamshire.

Garden house at Pollok House, Renfrew, by Sir Rowand Anderson; admirably placed as a stop
to two levels of terrace, stairway and wall.

A garden shelter of simple and charming classical design at Petwood, Woodhall Spa. By Mr. Harold Peto.

Stone summerhouse at Nailsea Court, Somerset.   A beautiful and interesting example.
Early Jacobean work.

Pavilion with pillared portico at Wrest Park, Bedfordshire.

Garden pavilion, seen from the middle plat at the Villa Rosemary, Alpes Maritimes. By Mr. Harold Peto.

Drayton House, Northamptonshire.   Garden house at the north-west angle of the
Italian garden.

18th century garden house at Charlton House, Kent.

A charming thatched summerhouse at an angle of the garden at Kelly House, Devonshire.

Garden loggia at Dogmersfield Park, Hampshire.

A suntrap garden house of unusual plan.

Tea room open on two sides at Grey Walls, Gullane, Scotland.

A pair of Kentish hop-oasts, converted, with addition, into a bothy at Godinton, by Mr. Reginald Blomfield.

The garden face of the same, forming a continuation of the garden wall.

Summerhouse at Apethorpe Hall, Northants, of Italian loggia design.

Garden pavilion, grouped with bridge and pool, at Hartham Park, Wiltshire.
By Mr. Harold Peto.

Two garden buildings connected by a loggia at Temple Dinsley, Hertfordshire. By Sir Edwin Lutyens.

Pavilion at the eastern angle of a flower garden at Montacute, Somerset.

The Queen's Building at Stowe. The grounds of this palatial place are plentifully adorned with temples, pavilions and memorial columns, placed at the ends of vistas or at the termination of artificial waters. Besides the great Rotunda of Vanbrugh, there are several temples designed by Kent, notably the Temple of Venus and the Temple of Ancient Virtues. The Queen's Building, once the Ladies' Temple, has an imposing flight of steps and a pedimented portico with fluted and otherwise ornate Corinthian columns and decorative accessories. These buildings were designed entirely for external effect, for they were never put to any useful purpose, although the interior of the Queen's Building is a room of some size and dignity, with columns at the sides supporting a rich cornice, above which the barrel-shaped ceiling has an enrichment of moulded panelling.

Interior of the Queen's Building, Stowe, Buckinghamshire.

Italian loggia with angle bastion, looking over the Thames valley at Cliveden, Bucks.

The Renaissance garden house at Margam Park, Glamorgan ; early
Jacobean ; a relic of the earlier house.

The Chinese temple summerhouse at Amesbury Abbey, Wilts.

A garden pavilion at King's Weston, Gloucestershire.

Holbein's porch, now a garden house, at Wilton House, Wiltshire. The only remaining portion of the original Tudor mansion.

North side of the pavilion, with statue of King William III, at Wrest Park, Bedfordshire.
Designed by Thomas Archer.

The Shakespeare temple in the grounds of Garrick's Villa at Hampton, Middlesex.

Garden temple in the grounds of The Villa Borghese, Rome.

A beautiful brick garden house at The Vyne, Hampshire, with four pedimented projections and a tiled dome.

Garden house at Melford Hall, Suffolk. The proportions are quite spoilt and details
entirely lost by overgrowth of Ivy and other creepers.

Long Wittenham, Berkshire. Summer-house with open side. By Mr. E. Guy Dawber. Many summer houses are useless as a quiet retreat for reading or writing because they have no side light, but here the wide opening not only gives another view of the garden and pergola, but a good light for reading.

An 18th century garden-house at the angle of walls. So good a building should be carefully guarded from any encroachment by ivy or ampelopsis, though a graceful wall plant, cleverly guided, may add to its beauty and do no harm.

Summer Farm, Surrey. A range of cow-houses converted into a loggia. By Sir Edwin Lutyens. Many sets of old farm buildings are now being arranged as adjuncts to dwelling houses, and resourceful architects are glad to take advantage of a long range of shedding for such a purpose as is here shown.

DOVECOTES

A large pigeon-house, circular in plan, at the angle of garden walls at Rousham, Oxfordshire.

Dovecote ending a return wall by the Iris pool at Barrow Court, Somersetshire

A tall circular pigeon-house.

Dovecote built as a tall square pier at Mr. Ernest Gimson's house, Sapperton, Glos.

Four-gabled pigeon-house at Chastleton House, Gloucestershire.

Circular dovecote at Athelhampton, Dorset.

A modern pump-house and dovecote.

Circular dovecote at Cleeve Prior Manor, Worcestershire.

Circular brick dovecote at Little Pednor Farm, Chesham. By Forbes & Tate.

Circular dovecote at Kyre Park, Worcestershire.

Dovecote built as a finish to the
end of a wall. By Inigo Triggs.

A four-gabled dovecote at Shipton Court,
Oxfordshire.

A remarkable old dovecote at Willington, Bedfordshire. The
crow-steps at the gables and in the middle line of the roof are
convenient perches for the pigeons.

Dovecote on a tall wooden post.
By J. P. White & Son.

Stone-built bee-house at Midmar
Castle, Scotland.

Thatched bee-house at Spetchley Park, Worcestershire.

PARTERRES

PARTERRES

IT was usual for the great houses to have an important parterre next to the wide terrace on the garden front. The effect was always best when the house and terrace stood on a higher level, so that access from the terrace to the parterre was gained by a flight of steps. In some cases, and always with excellent effect, the terrace returned forward at the two ends, so enclosing the sides of the garden, and the outer ends would be finished with an important garden house. In this way there were good views of the parterre from three sides, and still higher points of view from the pavilions.

The original prototype of the parterre was undoubtedly Italian, and Italian methods were closely followed, and have since been revived, in the gardens of the houses of the English Renaissance. Many of them show elaborate scroll work or arabesque, wrought in box alone, a perhaps too slavish imitation to be reasonably perpetuated in our gardens, for, whereas the many plants that we have for the filling of flower beds were unknown in the 15th and 16th centuries, we have now more than enough to choose from ; moreover, our northern climate makes the use of coloured flowers more desirable. Beautiful examples of the good treatment of parterres existed a few years ago at Castle Ashby, and it is to be hoped that the same tradition is maintained. They were delightfully planned for colour harmony, so that each department formed a satisfying picture. Such intelligent employment of the summer plants showed the best possible utilization of the bedding system, which, in these large parterres, was, and always is, absolutely in place ; for its purpose is the making of a good show in the late summer months when the great houses are fully occupied.

Scrolls of solid Box in the winter garden at Longleat, Wilts.

Edgings of Ivy and Lavender-cotton in the parterre at Lyme Hall, Cheshire.

The High White Garden at Drumlanrig Castle, Dumfries. The central portion has double borderings of white-leaved plants, with an outer framing of green in a carpet pattern

The parterres at Castle Ashby, Northants. These gardens are beautifully planted for colour.

The large box-edged garden at Hewell Grange, Worcestershire.

A section of a formal garden with solid scroll-work in clipped Box at Balcarres, Fifeshire.

The effect of these gardens, already sufficiently complicated, is by no means improved by the introduction of rows of sparkling spar. It often comes about that a garden has been burdened, or, as in this case, absolutely disfigured, by some such device, adopted in obedience to some passing fashion; it has gone on from one generation to another till the owners have come to consider it a tradition of the place and have retained it for that reason. But a bad tradition is unworthy of respect or retention, and it is to be hoped that, with the better knowledge of gardening that now prevails, a custom, originally founded on an error of taste, may be abolished.

A parterre at Castle Ashby, Northants. The fan-shaped forms are planted in shades of yellow and orange, and the whole garden is treated carefully for colour effect.

Stoneleigh Abbey, Warwickshire.   The box-edged garden between the house and the river.

A parterre with edgings of moulded stone at Thorpe Hall,
Northamptonshire.

The East Garden and Maze at Hatfield House, Herts.

The Box-edged Rose garden at Rousham, Oxfordshire.

Italian garden at Dalzell, Lanarkshire, with prominent Box edging.

Thick Box edging to a parterre at Stoke Rochford, Lincs.

A garden of Box scroll-work at Stoke Edith Park, Herefordshire.

SUNDIALS

SUNDIALS

A SUNDIAL is always welcome in pleasure ground, not only as a distinctive ornament, but as a link with the old garden of our Tudor ancestors. Although in these days, when everyone carries a watch and when clocks are many, it has all but lost its original purpose, yet it is still pleasant in summer days to read the time by the sun on an old dial. Properly speaking the dial is the horizontal plate with its gnomon only, the stone base being the part that forms the ornament in the garden landscape, but we are accustomed to call the whole thing a sundial, and the term is so convenient that it may well be generally used.

It may be assumed that the oldest of these are the original sundials of the Tudor gardens, the greater number of which were swept away when the landscape gardening of the 18th century became the fashion, and the old enclosed gardens were considered barbarous. No doubt the sundial would be the only thing that escaped destruction, and this may account for the many that now exist in gardens placed apparently hap-hazard, or at any rate without much consideration; for we find them as if lost in an expanse of grass, the baluster base coming straight out of the green without any vestige of the stone step or platform that they probably had in their original position; whereas one may be sure that in the old Tudor garden the sundial was the central object in the knotted garden or parterre, or at any rate formed some important rallying point in the garden design.

The general form of the sundial base in England was the baluster, round or square in section, plain or enriched with sculptured ornament. In Scotland the more usual form was a tall shaft with obelisk top; the indication of time being given by a number of faceted forms. In the 18th century the prevailing fashion for lead figures in garden decoration accounts for the use of the well-known kneeling slave as a sundial base. The figure is always interesting, and lead is one of the best materials for our climate, but if accuracy of timekeeping is regarded as important, it is not a suitable thing to use on account of its great weight tending to settle out of shape.

A tall monumental ten-sided sundial at Newbattle Abbey, Midlothian.

A faceted dial at Balcarres, Fifeshire.

Sundial on baluster base with a figure of Time, at Duncombe Park, Yorkshire.

Sundial on a base of square baluster shape with sculptured
enrichment at The Vyne, Basingstoke, Hants.

A beautiful base formed of a slender, spirally-beaded column supported
by three angular brackets at Normanton Park, Rutland.

Sundial on a slender shaft, fluted and enriched with ornament of masks and drapery at Blickling Hall, Norfolk. It much wants a stone platform or step.

A facet-headed sundial at Melville House, Fife.

A wall dial on a square head mounted on a plain column over a well at Blaise Castle,
Gloucestershire.

Sundial on a baluster base, well placed in the gardens of Hampton Court.

Sundial on a baluster base enriched with a sculptured garland and acanthus leaves, at Blenheim Palace, Oxfordshire. It would be much improved by an additional step or platform.

Sundial on circular baluster base, standing on a suitable step, at Crichel, Dorset.

A square stone base with four bracket-shaped supports at Hinwick Hall, Bedfordshire.

Sundial on a vase-shaped base, richly sculptured with lions' heads and garlands. This important piece much wants a stone platform. At Amesbury Abbey, Wiltshire.

Sundial at the Deanery Garden, Sonning.   By Sir Edwin Lutyens.
The shaft has a spiral ornament inlaid with lead. It stands on an
adequate step on a square of pavement.

Sundial carried by a charming modern boy figure at Hartham Park, Wiltshire, in a garden
designed by Mr. Harold Peto.

Sundial on a circular base of Roman altar form, with sculptured wreath. It stands well on two moulded steps. At Newburgh Priory, Yorkshire.

Sundial on octagonal baluster base on a proper stone platform, at Wrest Park, Bedfordshire.

Sundial on a stone table supported by the lead figure of the kneeling negro slave; 18th century. At Glemham, Suffolk.

Armillary sphere dial at Kingston Lacy, Dorset.

Spherical dial at Minley Manor, Hampshire.

Sundial in the garden of Tythrop House,
Oxfordshire. The richly decorated baluster
base badly needs a supporting step.

Sundial at Chicheley Hall, Buckinghamshire,
standing on a stone pier.

Stone figure of Time bearing a sundial.

Leaden figure of kneeling slave bearing a sundial, at Aldenham House, Herts.

Faceted sundial with obelisk top, dated 1630, in the garden at Drummond Castle, Perthshire.

Vertical sundial on high stone steps at Formakin, Forfarshire. By Sir Robert Lorimer.

Sundial at Belton House, Lincolnshire. The base is supported by beautifully modelled figures of Time with an amorino. It stands well, on an adequate step and platform in the middle of a long walk.

A modern vertical dial on a Doric shaft at Woodside, Rickmansworth.

Sundial with 18th century baluster base at Ham
House, Richmond.

An old mortar at Culzean Castle, Ayrshire.

Sundial at Oulton Park, Cheshire, on a curious base of four slender
bulb-shaped columns ; 17th century.

Sundial on a slender baluster base at Hinchingbrooke, Hunts.

Sundial on a graceful, spirally fluted baluster base at Hatfield House, Herts.

TOPIARY WORK

TOPIARY WORK

MANY are the relics of topiary work in the older of our gardens, and though much of it has evidently become distorted from the shapes originally intended, yet enough of a comprehensible form remains to show how gladly our ancestors availed themselves of the docility of some kinds of evergreens. The wonderful green walls of yew at Sudeley Castle and Rockingham show what can be done, not only to ensure shelter, but to gain a kind of architectural expression, and many are the later examples where stone and tree, alike moulded into form, are obedient to the designer's hand. Even where they have gone quite astray, as in the curious garden at Levens, designed originally by a French artist in the reign of James II., the many yews, clipped into numerous fantastic forms, such as could never have been originally designed, give the old garden a rare charm, though it is a charm of a whimsical and freakish character. The splendid old yew hedge at Holme Lacy, like a weather-worn rock of vegetation, the surface clipped and yet showing something of its natural anatomy, is full of delightful interest, and in the same fine old garden other yew hedges, of lesser height but of many years' growth, form the best possible background to borders of hardy flowers.

In more than one of the gardens of the great Palladian houses there are walls of yew with circular-headed niches for the reception of sculpture, one of the best ways of placing sculpture in our gardens. In some of the old manor house gardens there stand rows of stately yews, each tree at a certain height stretching to right and left to meet its fellow, so forming a series of great green archways in order that each arch may give a different view of some aspect of garden beauty.

There are the two forms of topiary work, the one where the purpose is to make walls for shelter and for some kind of architectural expression, and the other which is purely ornamental—a survival or revival of the old way of shaping growing trees into figures of birds and beasts or of twisting spiral or of rounded forms one over another, looking as if they had been fashioned in a turner's lathe. These tricks and toys may easily be overdone, and it may be wise to restrain the shaped work to some points that call for punctuation, where a green ball or pyramid or obelisk may be rightly in place and, above all, where it is done by a designer who has an accurate sense of proportion.

Yew is the tree most usually employed for topiary work, but Box is also excellent and for walls or close hedges, Holly, Cypress, as well as the homely Privet. Laurel is a possible shrub for a large, tall hedge but requires special care in trimming ; it must all be done by hand, not with the shears, for a laurel leaf cut straight across is an unsightly mutilated object. Laurel, moreover, has the drawback of becoming somewhat " leggy " at its base.

Clipped Yew hedges at Holme Lacy, Herefordshire, forming backgrounds to flower-borders.

The hedge of ancient Yews at Holme Lacy, Herefordshire.

Shaped hedge and bee-hive Yews at Sudeley Castle, Gloucestershire.

The great wall of Yew, with central bastion, arches, and loop-holes at Sudeley Castle, Gloucestershire.

The double row of Yew pyramids at Brickwall Sussex.

Green wall linking the piers at Gayhurst, Buckinghamshire. The clipping would be improved by keeping the portion next the piers quite level and just below the cornice, so that the whole succession of cornices is visible.

Some of the curious forms of clipped Yews in the old garden at Levens Hall, Westmorland.

The great clipped Yews, called the twelve apostles, at Cleeve Prior Manor, Worcestershire.

Yews clipped to careful design in the garden at Blickling Hall, Norfolk.

Yew hedge with six entrance arches, surrounding the circular Rose Garden at Rockingham Castle, Northamptonshire.

Yews clipped in the form of turned finials in the garden at Bradfield, Devon.

Curiously shaped Yews in the Rose Garden at Chastleton House, Gloucestershire.

Topiary buttresses at the foot of a balustraded retaining wall at Balcarres, Fife.

Well kept clipped hedges and pyramidal Yews in the garden at Crathes Castle, Aberdeenshire.

Clipped Yews at Owlpen Manor, Gloucestershire.

The great clipped Yews at St. Catherine's Court, near Bath.

Yew hedges at Henbury Court, Gloucestershire ; clipped as if to suggest a roofed wall.

Clipped Yews with Egyptian doorway and guardian Sphinxes at Biddulph Grange, Cheshire.

Yew hedges at Wickham Court, Kent.

Ancient Yews at Hall Barn, Buckinghamshire.

A formal green garden with fountain centre and dwarf clipped hedges of square section at Honington Hall, Warwickshire.

A portion of the curious topiary work at Levens Hall, Westmorland.

Some excellent topiary work at Brockenhurst Park, Hampshire. The niches are well proportioned to the sculptures.

A green garden at Condover Hall, Shropshire, with dwarf clipped hedges.

Dwarf green hedge to a paved formal garden at Balcaskie, Fifeshire, between the house and the balustrade of the great retaining wall.

Shaped yews, flanking a sundial, at Brickwall, Sussex.

PERGOLAS AND TREILLAGE

THE PERGOLA

WHILE in the older days of gardening every kind of ornament and accessory was borrowed from Italy, it seems a strange thing that it should be only in recent years that we have adopted the pergola, a feature that has added so greatly to the beauty and interest of our pleasure grounds. And though its original purpose was the support of vines only, yet it need not have taken centuries for us to perceive how conveniently it could be adapted to flowering plants of climbing habit or to see how its structure could be suited to every kind and degree of gardening, from the highest expression of architectural refinement, as shown in the work of Mr. Harold Peto in the south of France as well as at home, to the simplest erection of posts or even poles, in the garden of an English cottage.

A permanent structure, especially as to the piers, is highly desirable ; whether they are to be of brick or stone, or, as so often in Italy, and always with good effect, of rough rubble coarsely plastered, must be decided by the character of the house and garden and the local material most suitably available. The pairs of piers should be tied across the path with a stout beam of oak or larch slightly cambered ; the upward curve, if even quite slight, gives a satisfying look of strength, and is in fact a source of strength, resisting the pressure of the slighter wood which forms the roof.

It is usual for a pergola to be continuous, but if it is to be for roses it is better that it should be of a succession of piers and beams only, for in this way the roses have the benefit of light and air all round. Roses are not so suitable for the all covered pergola. As to the best plants, grape vines are always beautiful, although ripe fruit cannot be expected. Aristolochia, Wistaria and Virginia Creeper are excellent, White Jasmine, and many of the Clematises, both of the species and of the large garden hybrids. A whole covered way of Laburnum has been made with great success. In the old days the nearest approach to the idea and purpose of the pergola was the pleached alley of the Tudor gardens, when young trees of Hornbeam or Wych-elm were trained over a tunnel-shaped trellis of laths. Such pleached alleys or covert ways were planted all through Tudor and Stuart days, and examples still remain of some, as at Drayton and Hampton Court, that were presumably planted either at the extreme end of the 17th or the beginning of the 18th century.

TREILLAGE

IT would appear that the elaborate pavilions and arcades of complicated treillage of the 17th and 18th centuries might be a natural evolution, through many intervening stages of progress, from the older pleached alleys. But as the later woodwork became more highly wrought, essential differences came to be apparent. For in the case of the pleached alley the woodwork was temporary and of secondary consideration ; it was only strong and enduring enough to serve as a scaffolding on which the growing trees were to be trained, and might be discarded or suffered to disappear by natural decay when the growth had covered it and had completed the form intended. The later treillage had another purpose ; it was carefully designed as garden architecture, and though it might be partly covered with flowering plants, it was not to be smothered, but was always to show, not only its main structure but the greater part of its detail. In some cases the whole was covered with Ivy, but eventually such a purpose was entirely lost sight of and the elaborate edifice, with its arches and pinnacles, domes and pediments was considered so sacred that no planting might invade it. Happily we have now returned to a saner and more moderate use of treillage, and the illustrations show some recent work designed by Mr. Peto, where the finely designed wooden structure and the nobler of the flowering plants appear in their just relation, and form a satisfying and properly balanced complement one to the other.

The system of cordon and espalier fruit trees might well be adapted to some form of treillage a little better than the usual post and wire. Where flower borders pass through a large kitchen garden, such a treillage would be an excellent background to the flowering plants. It has been done with success at Orchards in Surrey, and the good example should be followed and further developed.

Pergola at the Capuchin Convent, Amalfi.

The great rubble and plaster columns of the pergola at the Capuchin Convent, Amalfi.

Some beautiful modern work by Mr. Harold Peto at the Villa Rosemary, Alpes Maritimes.

The pergola of tall Ionic columns at Isola Bella, Cannes. By Mr. Harold Peto. A corresponding length of curved pergola swings round to the central Temple, enclosing a pool.

The Temple end of the curved pergola at Isola Bella, Cannes.   The work of Mr. Harold Peto.

Pergola and steps at the Villa Rosemary, Alpes Maritimes.

One side of the curved pergola on Ionic columns at Isola Bella, Cannes.

A vine pergola of slight poles in Mrs. F. Eden's garden in Venice.

Pergola with treillage at Little Thakeham, Sussex.   By Sir Edwin Lutyens.

An alley in the pergola garden at Mounton House, Chepstow.   By Mr. H. Avray Tipping.

Pergola piers of solid stone in the paved pool garden at Mounton House, Chepstow.
By Mr. H. Avray Tipping.

The Rose pergola at Mounton House, Chepstow.   By Mr. H. Avray Tipping.

A pergola of rough posts such as requires frequent repair and renewal.

A pergola of vines on oak posts and beams and open treillage of wooden rods forming a covered way to the stables at Gravetye Manor, Sussex. The walls are full of spring flowering plants that bloom before the vine leaves shade the path.

Substantial and well-designed treillage.   When the plants are trained on such work as this it is important that they should avoid covering such points as the caps and parts of the shafts of columns, the urn finials and the main lines of the arches.

Irrigation channel and vine pergola on posts of plastered rubble, at the Villa Mahieddin, Algiers

A pergola well-built with solid wrought stone piers and oak beams at Buckhurst Park, Sussex.

A solidly built pergola at Hestercombe, Somersetshire.

A well-made pergola with posts of fourteen inch brickwork and wrought oak beams at the Deanery Garden, Sonning.

Pergola on rising ground with solid piers and wide stone steps at Notgrove Manor, Glos.   The top is of rough branches laid " rustic " fashion.

A pergola of brick pillars round and square.

Pergola with round and square brick pillars at the Deanery Garden, Sonning.

Treillage with classical columns at Bridge House, Weybridge.   By Mr Harold Peto.

Arched treillage with domed centre at Easton Lodge, Essex. By Mr. Harold Peto.

A detail of the arched treillage at Easton Lodge, Essex.

The arched treillage at Easton Lodge, Essex, from within.

Architectural treillage at Warren Towers, Newmarket, not intended to be covered.

Pergola with treillage front. The lines of the outer arches should not be too much covered.

A pleached alley of old fruit trees at Drayton House, Northamptonshire.

Fruit trees on an iron framework, forming a continous gallery, at Broad Oaks, Surrey.

A long alley of fruit trees on a framework of wood and iron at Lilleshall, Shropshire.

Oak trellis for fruit trees at the back of a flower border in a kitchen garden.

An arbour of trellis work, the walls to be covered with climbing plants.

A colonnade pergola, with dome at an important view point, at Rankeilour, Fifeshire.

Colonnade and pavilion of treillage at Cornbury Park, Oxfordshire.

A wall-top treated as a pergola.

Plain trellis for climbing plants on a
Manchester house front.

A structure of wooden posts and iron trellis, passing through a kitchen garden at Dunchurch
Lodge, Rugby.   The fruit trees on the screen at the back of the flower border will effectually
hide the vegetable ground and glasshouses.

Pergola piers at Crooksbury, Surrey; fourteen inches by nine at the base, thinning buttress fashion to nine by nine at two-thirds of the height, and thinning again at the actual seating of the beam.

Treillage in a hillside garden, Bodnant, Denbighshire.

A stepped pergola at Acremead, Kent. Designed by Dunbar Smith and Cecil Brewer.

The upper part of the pergola at Acremead, Kent.

Tool-house combined with pergola at Highmount, Surrey.

Plain wall trelliage at the Maison de Sylvie, Chantilly.

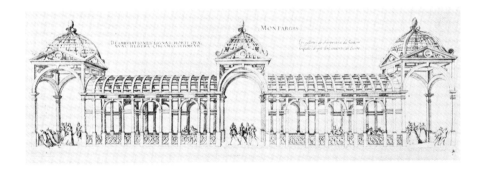

Gallery of wooden treillage connecting domed pavilions in the garden at Montarges.

Wooden treillage of obelisk form at the Ile d'Amour in the Park, Chantilly.

The Temple de l'Amour, Chantilly.   A remarkable example
of elaborate French treillage.

Pergola pillars of round and square section built of thin brick; at Tigbourne Court, Surrey.

CANALS, PONDS, AND WATER GARDENS

CANALS, PONDS AND WATER GARDENS

THE straight, canal shaped pieces of water that exist in many large places are commonly considered to be the outcome of Dutch influence in the time of William and Mary. But their prototype or perhaps contemporary, the great canal at Hampton Court, was of an earlier date, for it was formed in the time of Charles II., if not from the actual design, at least under the immediate influence of the great French garden architect Le Nôtre, whose example, founded on his recent extensive works at Versailles, became a guiding motive to garden designers throughout England. Following this and in connexion with the more extended views of the landscape gardeners of the 18th century, large pools and ponds were formed, rivers were widened or their courses were altered in order to gain good views of water from the house, and from such time onwards, water, when reasonably available, has always taken its part in our schemes of garden delight.

A further incitement to the use of water has been provided by the many forms and colours of waterlilies now so easily to be had ; and it is only when a pool is quite small and is used chiefly for dipping, that these and other beautiful aquatic plants cannot be so conveniently employed. Even where there is only the least thread of running water it can be turned to account by a narrow stone bordered rill that can be easily stepped over, with tiny pools at intervals, as at Sonning and Hestercombe. A matter of some importance that is too often overlooked is that the water in pools or tanks should be kept at the right level, and that the level should be kept as high as may be with regard to a practical overflow. If a dipping tank does not automatically fill itself by a constant natural feed, the water should be turned on to make good as soon as possible, or while the dipping is going on. Nothing looks more neglected than a half empty tank.

The water garden at Marsh Court, Hampshire. By Sir Edwin Lutyens.

The enclosed water-garden at King's Weston, Gloucestershire. The absence of any parapet or planting next to the water gives a slight apprehension of danger in this delightfully planned and charming garden.

A quiet garden pool at Holme Lacy, Herefordshire. The whole effect gains much by the great trees and their reflection in the water.

A square pool and narrow rill in the water garden at the Deanery Garden, Sonning.   By Sir Edwin Lutyens.

The lily pool in the water garden at Bridge House, Weybridge, as seen from the garden house. By Mr. Harold Peto.

The water garden at Bridge House, Weybridge, looking to the garden house.

The water garden at Bridge House, Weybridge. Shallow places are built for the benefit of water Plantain and other aquatic plants that grow only just under water.

The Italian water garden at Easton Lodge, Essex. By Mr. Harold Peto.

A long canal at Westbury Court, Gloucestershire.

The great pool at Westbury Court, Gloucestershire, with a figure of a Triton and dolphin on a stone plinth set in the water.

Part of the water garden and bridge from within the pavilion at Hartham Park, Wiltshire.
By Mr. Harold Peto.

A moat end with buttresses bearing large pots of Agapanthus, at Crowhurst, Sussex.

The long lily pool and pavilion at Hartham Park, Wilts. The edge of the pavement where it joins the raised curb is pleasantly planted.

A water court at Hestercombe, Somersetshire. By Sir Edwin Lutyens. This example shows the good effect of the high water-level.

The garden pool at Athelhampton, Dorsetshire.

The stepped canal at Buscot Park, Berkshire

Buscot Park, Berkshire. The lower pool garden, looking south

Balustraded embankment and landing steps to the Avon at Stoneleigh Abbey, Warwickshire.

Long canal and pool at Bicton, Devonshire.

The pool, with the canal on a slightly lower level, at Bicton, Devonshire.

The pond garden at Newstead Abbey, Nottinghamshire.

One end of the rectangular pool, above the canal at Bicton, Devonshire.

A beautiful pond garden at Westbury Court, Gloucestershire.

A water garden by Sir Edwin Lutyens at Hestercombe, Somerset

A quiet circular basin at Melbourne, Derbyshire, with the lead figure of Mercury designed by John of Bologna.

Pool in the enclosed garden at Athelhampton Hall, Dorset ; with three slender jets of water.

Stone-edged basin with water jet and high Yew hedges at Palace House, Beaulieu, Hampshire.

Rectangular pond edged with Yew hedges at Ashridge Park, Hertfordshire.

In the pond garden at King's Weston, Gloucestershire.

Fountain basin with four stone lions and central pillar at Formakin, Renfrewshire.
By Sir Robert Lorimer.

One of the upper pools at Buscot Park, Berkshire.

Balustraded fountain pool at Frascati.

The turn of the walled moat at Crowhurst, Sussex.

A sunk water garden of rectangular form with planted outer retaining walls, at
Crowhurst, Sussex.

Another view of the water garden at Crowhurst, Sussex.

BRIDGES

BRIDGES

URING the 17th and 18th centuries architects took advantage of the need of bridges in the grounds of palatial houses to erect structures of some magnificence. The type of roofed bridge with pedimented ends showing three ways, and an imposing façade of Ionic columns to each water-front, that we know as Palladian, was first built in England either by Inigo Jones himself or under his direct influence, and was from time to time repeated during the next hundred and fifty years by Vanbrugh and the brothers Adam ; the design remaining unaltered but for slight variation of scale, proportion or decorative detail. Within the same period many fine stone bridges were built for smaller places of the best class, with balustraded parapets ; the more ornate having decorative sculptures of urn or figure surmounting the piers.

Throughout the country on the public roads there are stone bridges some hundreds of years old, many of them of rude construction, but full of character and of the kind of beauty that comes of a thing simply done with the material nearest to hand to fulfil a local need. Some of these bridges have stone-walled parapets ; in some cases the parapet breaks forward into a bay, formed by the projecting pier being carried up ; so providing a place of safety for foot passengers from passing waggons often widely loaded. Others have a strong railing of oak, with support given by projecting beams built into the masonry and a brace mortised and pinned to beam and post.

The wooden bridges, of which, in these days of ponderous traffic, so few remain, were also built in a simple and delightful way ; and much to be regretted are the many little footbridges over stream and small river that still abounded in the earlier part of the 19th century, and that old people may still remember. It is interesting to notice, where an old bridge crosses a river, that there is nearly always clear evidence of a still older ford ; the bottom being made shallow and stony, and sometimes necessarily widened. It is sad to see, throughout the country, the many examples of quite needless ugliness that present themselves in the cast iron and other atrocities that now replace the beautiful bridges of the older days.

The stone bridge at Cowdray Park, Sussex.

Balustraded bridge at Stoke Park, Buckinghamshire.

Balustraded bridge of classical design at Amesbury Abbey, Wiltshire.

The Palladian bridge at Wilton House, Wiltshire. By a pupil of Inigo Jones.

The Palladian bridge at Stowe House, Buckinghamshire.

The bridge at Blenheim Palace, Oxfordshire.   By Vanbrugh.

Balustraded bridge and weir at Kedleston Hall, Derbyshire.

Bridge across the moat at Leeds Castle, Kent.

Masonry bridge at Tyringham, Bucks. By Sir John Soane, R.A., 1795.

The Maiden Bridge at Newbattle Abbey, Midlothian.

Eashing Bridge.   One of several bridges of the same character that
cross the Wey in south-west Surrey.

Bridge at Grasmere, by Mr. Mawson, well suited to its position on a rocky hillside.

Brick bridge in ornamental ground at Wrest Park, Bedfordshire.

Bridge at Rowallan, Ayrshire.

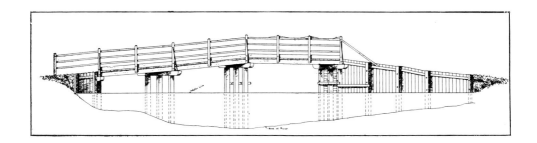

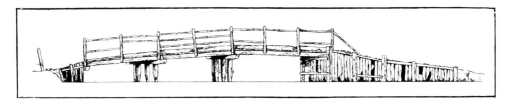

Elevation and sketch of Flatford Bridge.

Flatford Bridge.   An excellent type of wooden bridge of the simplest construction.

A simple stone bridge over a stream in wild ground.

Wooden bridge at Mounton House, Chepstow.   By Mr. H. Avray Tipping.

The stone bridge at Iford Manor, Wiltshire.

The fine stone bridge at Chiswick House with beautiful urns on the piers, all cruelly overgrown
with Ivy.

The bridge at Chiswick House with the overgrowth removed.

Another view of the bridge at Chiswick House, cleared of its former overgrowth.

Castle Eaton Bridge on the Upper Thames. Typical of the old country bridges and of the way of supporting the railing.

The seven-arched bridge over the Arun at Stopham, Sussex.

A stone bridge in the water garden at Buscot Park, Berkshire.

FOUNTAINS AND DIPPING

WELLS

FOUNTAINS AND DIPPING WELLS

THE fountains in the old gardens of Italy are those that we think of as the finest examples of the use of water in pleasure grounds, and, though the immense waterworks of Versailles may out-do them as to mere size and engineering efficiency, yet the merit for the best use of water for the charm and delight of mankind must ever remain with Italy. It is specially satisfactory in the case of some of the villas at Frascati on the slopes of the Alban hills, some fifteen miles from Rome. Here water is naturally in abundance, and a whole copious stream can be used to form a water stair, while the retention of a bulk of water on a high level provides by its weight and natural gravitation for the jets of noble fountains on a lower level. Others of the old villas are at Tivoli in the Sabine hills, also within easy reach of Rome, where there are the remains of the great villa of Hadrian, and water is again in abundance. Here is the Villa d'Este, with its superb avenue of ancient cypresses, its terraces and noble stairway and its varied play of many waters.

Sculptured ornament has always figured prominently in connexion with fountains, either alone or combined with architectural form. Colossal river-gods, with shells or urns from which whole small rivers pour forth, Tritons with dolphins, and figure subjects from ancient mythology are frequent and familiar examples ; some of them have come to our own gardens as we see in the case of the graceful figure of Mercury, the work of John of Bologna.

Travellers are well acquainted with the dipping wells in Venice with their handsome heads of sculptured stone ; some with wrought-iron supports for a pulley and chain, others without, where the women, with a few yards of rope, pull up their copper buckets by hand.

The Fountain of the Dragons at the Villa d'Este, Tivoli.

The Cascade of the Fountain of the Organ at the Villa d'Este, Tivoli. This, among the many waters of the Villa d'Este, indicates the lavish use that was made of the power and volume of an inexhaustible and constant water supply. It is said that a whole river was diverted to feed the many fountains, pools, jets, and miniature torrents, whose sight and sound contribute so greatly to the charm and delight of this wonderful garden.

The great balustraded fountain pool at the Villa Conti, Frascati.

A raised fountain basin at the Villa Albani, Rome, standing on a pavement of fine but very simple concentric design.

The Cloister Fountain at Newstead Abbey, Nottinghamshire.

The four-square water garden at the Villa Lante, Italy, with large central fountain.

Fountain pier and balustrade with stone seats at Cliveden, Buckinghamshire.   Formerly at
the Villa Borghese, Rome.

Fountain basin with a beautiful tazza of Belgian black marble and figure group by Mr. John Hughes. The curb has eight bronze tortoises on half-round balls that spurt into the basin. Heywood, Queen's County, Ireland.

Dipping pool of St. Tivisian, at Landivisian, Brittany.

Well in the courtyard at Meillant, Cher, France.

Well with pillared cupola of French Renaissance design, in a courtyard at Verjean, Brittany.

Well in a courtyard at the Chateau de Chenonceau, Indre-et-Loire, France.

A fine architectural treatment of a pond-head with wall fountains, at Cowley Manor,
Gloucestershire.

Dipping tank in the Deanery Garden, Sonning.

Lily tank in the Deanery Garden, Sonning.

Fountain in the Deanery Garden, Sonning

Wall fountain and dipping pool at Hampton Court Palace.

Italy.

Wall jet and basin at Hillingdon House, near Cromer.

Dipping pool at Hestercombe, Somerset, fed by a spouting mask.

Fountain with colossal water gods and raised basin of elongated sarcophagus form at the Villa Lante, near Viterbo Italy.

The Mercury fountain at Madresfield Court, Worcestershire.

The long rill, fed by many wall spouts, at the Villa d'Este, Tivoli.

Fountain forming the centre of a design of wide grass paths and flower borders at Crowhurst, Sussex.

Fountain tazza at Chateau Anet, Eure-et-Loire, France.

A square dipping tank.　　　　　A water basin in a terrace wall.

Wall fountain at Orchards, Godalming ; the　water spouts from a
lion's head mask modelled by Lady Chance.

Dipping well in the kitchen garden at Orchards, Godalming.

Basin in the open central court at Papillon Hall, Leicestershire.

Dipping pool in the North garden, Campagne
Mahieddin, Algiers.

Court of the Hareem, Campagne Mahieddin, Algiers. The tiles set in zig-zag panels above
the columns and in the horizontal course just under the eaves, are not Arab but Dutch;
captured in Dutch ships by Algerine pirates.

An Arab puzzle fountain and birds' drinking place of the Campagne Mahieddin, Algiers.

The fountain court, Djenan-el-Mufti, Algiers.

A garden court in the Generalife, Granada ; looking southward from the northern portico.

The Canal Court in the Generalife, Granada ; looking westward.

Dipping and filling fountain at the Palazzo Bevilaqua, Bologna, fed by the Lion of Bramantino.

Dipping pool at Bodnant, Denbighshire.

FLOWER BORDERS

FLOWER BORDERS

A FLOWER border is seen to the best advantage when it has some solid backing such as a wall or an evergreen hedge. Perhaps the wall is the better of the two, as it may also be covered with flowering plants. On the other hand, the rich, dark green of a hedge of Yew or Holly is a noble background to bright flowers. It has only the disadvantage that the roots quickly invade the flower border, and that a foot or two of space should be left for the convenience of clipping in summer. The proper kind of edging has also to be considered. If the flowers are close to the house, with near forms that are straight and rectangular, borders will probably be edged with Box, especially if the path or terrace is of gravel or flagstones ; for though Box is not necessary where a border adjoins Flags, yet it helps towards a well-dressed appearance, and its strong line, with a certain primness, may be well in character with a house of 18th century or older type. When there is Box edging, small plants are not used at the front, and it may be found advisable to have an admixture of bushy growths, such as Lavender, Rosemary, hardy Fuchsia, and bush Roses, among the softer herbaceous plants. Where the flower borders are further from the house it is well to edge them with stone, so that the smaller plants of trailing habit may run over them at will.

But borders are, perhaps, best of all when they are at the sides of lawns, and the grass comes to the edge of the flowers. In this case the space of lawn next to the border should be mown with a hand grass-hook, so that any large-leaved plant, such as a Megasea or a Funkia, so handsome in such a position, should not have any leaves that may overlap the grass injured by the machine.

Delphiniums in the hardy flower border with Eschscholtzia and Sweet Alyssum to the front.

Flowers borders in the late Canon Swayne's garden at Salisbury.

Broad grass path with double flower border at Compton Wynyates, Warwickshire.

Hardy plants backed by Yew hedges at Balcarres, Fifeshire.

Hardy flowers in large masses at Compton Wynyates, Warwickshire.

Rose garden and flower borders at Abbotswood, Gloucestershire.

A wide border of Pentstemons at Claremont Park, Surrey.

Flower border along the terrace wall at Hardwick Hall, Derbyshire.

Flower border and planted drywalling at Abbotswood, Gloucestershire.

Grass fronted flower border screening the kitchen garden, at Harrowden Hall, Northants.

Borders of Cannas and other tender summer flowers at Penrhyn Castle, Carnarvonshire.

Climbing Rose on a brick pier by the moat at Crowhurst, Sussex.

Wall-backed flower borders at Arley Hall, Cheshire.

A torrent of Rambling Roses pouring over dry walling.

Grass path with narrow borders backed by yew hedges at Holme Lacy, Herefordshire.

Borders of hardy flowers in a North London garden.

Wide grass path with double flower border backed by a Holly hedge at Bulwick Hall, Northants.

By the side of the moat, Crowhurst, Sussex.

Wide grassy ways with flower borders at Crowhurst, Sussex.

Flower borders divided into compartments by projections of clipped Yew.   The rigid formality of this treatment would be bettered if completed by a Box edging next the pavement, that would carry on the front line of the yews.   Earlshall, Fife.

A high Yew hedge with buttresses of the same, dividing the border into separate compartments; at Biddulph Grange, Cheshire.

High wall and gateway with shaped Yew buttresses and wide grass verge to a flower border at Arley Hall, Cheshire, where there is much beautiful gardening.

Galtonia in the flower borders at Levens Hall, Westmorland.

Bellflowers and Foxgloves, with Pinks next the grass path, at Harleyford, Buckinghamshire.

Rambling Rose Thalia on an old apple tree.

Flower borders with paved paths.

Rose Mme. Alfred Carrière, covering an old espalier stump.

Box-edged flower borders at Campsea Ash, Suffolk.

Flower borders in the kitchen garden at Orchards, Surrey.

Rambling rose on an entrance pier.

Hardy flowers in border and dry walling.

Yuccas in the flower border.

Plants in pots on a raised step in a paved court.

Grey, purple, pink, and white in an August flower border.

A low wall, planted on the top, face, and at foot.

A border of hardy flowers—Delphiniums, Campanulas, and Snapdragons,
with Rose pillars at back.

A southward-facing flower border.

A well-grown pillar Rose.

WALL GARDENING

WALL GARDENING

IT is of comparatively recent years that we have learnt how much may be done by planting in the joints of retaining walls, in steps and the edges of pavements. There is hardly any garden plant that does well in a flower border that will not do as well—in some cases much better—in a wall, and many tender plants that would perish in the open escape by being planted well in between the stones, where their crowns are appreciably protected. Planting in rough stone steps and pavements —the later especially—is often overdone ; the planting should never interfere with the use of either, and should be mainly restricted to the edges, so as to give the impression that the plants had sprung from seed shattered by those growing near, rather than from having been deliberately planted.

Where ground is steep and parallel terraces follow one another with but little space between, it is best to give the space for planting on the flat to the upper side so that the path may pass close to the foot of the wall, the better to observe and enjoy the plants in the actual wall joints ; and it will be found to add much, not only to the good effect, but to the general cohesion of the arrangement, if, combined with any group of plants in the upper joints there are some of the same in the flat planting space above, so that the whole thing groups together.

Any local stone is good for dry-walling, and it is better than brick because the irregularity of the pieces provides larger openings for the plants ; but brick, with earth joints, can also be used with success.

It is not by any means small plants only that are fit for dry-walling, for Mulleins, Foxgloves, and Columbines are among the best, especially if they are grown directly from seed in the joint ; and many bushy and half bushy things succeed admirably.

An old wall with plants in the upper joints and with opportunities for further planting.

Drywalling in the early stages of planting, at Hestercombe, Somerset.

High retaining walls, well clothed, at Clevedon Court, Somerset.

A waved wall at Heveningham Hall, Suffolk. Such walls were built in order to catch more sun and to lengthen the planting space.

Terraces at Gilling Castle, Yorkshire, with fruit trees on the retaining walls and flower borders at the foot.

Wall with circular niches for sculpture, backing the pergola, at Heywood,
Queen's County, Ireland.   By Sir Edwin Lutyens.

Heywood, Queen's County, Ireland.   Steps from the oval garden to the
upper terrace, east of the house.

One of two old Dublin milestones, used as ornaments in the garden at Heywood, Queen's County, Ireland.

Terraces at Heywood, Queen's County, Ireland, from the pavilion door to the oval garden. The pavilion is too much obscured by climbing plants.

Brick dry walling planted with early summer flowers.

Mounting block and entrance piers clothed with Rambling Roses.

A planted wall at Villa Maryland, Alpes Maritimes, France.

A planted dry wall with Lupins and Irises, and Pinks at the foot.

Paved terrace with flower borders and retaining walls.

Heywood, Queen's County, Ireland. An opening in the curved wall of the oval garden leading to the yew garden, which is an old garden renewed.

Scotch Briar on a dry wall.

Cerastium on a buttressed dry wall.

The growth of Ampelopsis on a fine old
house, cleverly restrained.

Phlomis, Foxglove and Stonecrop planted
in the dry wall.

Mullein in dry walling.

Rock pinks in the joints of dry walling.

A Devonshire Wall of "Cob," with thatched coping. Cob is a sort of
concrete of rammed earth that has long been used for walling in some
of the south-western counties.

Heywood, Queen's County, Ireland. A high retaining wall enclosing the new garden,
by Sir Edwin Lutyens: from the further side of the upper lake.

The white Italian Campanula (C. isophylla alba)
in the wall at Highmount, Guildford.

This handsome wall is planted rather too much all over.

Combined planting of face and top in a low dry wall.

Retaining wall planted with Catmint, Iberis, Pinks, etc.

An old wall covered with flowering growth at Traquair House, Peeblesshire.

A 16th century wall, with Pinks and other flowering plants in the coping.

JAPANESE GARDENS

JAPANESE GARDENS

IT is difficult for anyone with western ideas of horticulture to be able to appreciate justly the wonderful gardens of Japan. For though they entirely set aside our aims of symmetry and definite planning and go wholly to Nature for their inspiration, yet, although the result is entirely natural, it is also intensely artificial; the consciousness of artifice being only lost in the case of the ancient rocks and groves of the old conventual buildings, where, in the course of ages, the influences of Nature have re-asserted themselves.

The rules of garden design in Japan, through the many centuries during which the art has been practised, have become codified into a kind of horticultural dogma. They have their origin in a gradually growing tradition, some branches of it based on history, religion, and philosophy. Imagination, inspired by suggestion, answers frequent appeals, and the whole thing is full of subtleties only to be apprehended by a mind already saturated with a knowledge of Japanese historical, poetical, and traditional procedure. Though advantage is taken of anything desirable that may exist on the site, such as a distant view, a rocky bank or a hillock in middle distance, some of this if non-existent can be made ; but if water is desired but is absent, it is hinted at. A stream of water-washed pebbles suggests a running brook, and an expanse of beaten earth, kept quite free from weeds, or of clean sand raked into ripples, gives the idea of a pool of water. But many of the best gardens of Japan have water, of which admirable use is made, with its accompaniment of flowering plants and its carefully constructed rocky shore. Throughout these gardens, so vividly does the mind of the designer seize upon the suitable treatment, though always within the prescribed rules, and so keen is his appreciation of matters of proportion, poise, balance, and all the qualities that make for beauty, that even to the uninitiated western eye these gardens are full of charm. The secret of this charm may probably be attributed to the modesty of the whole aim ; to that reverence and admiration for what is best in Nature, which has been the designer's constant and carefully fostered sentiment, and of which his finished work is the elaborated expression.

We learn from Professor Conder's illuminating treatise that there are three distinct styles of garden design, and that the details of any one style may never be combined with that of another in any one composition, though the style chosen may be so modified or treated as to convey some sentiment or abstract idea in keeping with the character or tastes of the owner. Various are the means of producing these modifications. In the use of rocks and stones alone there is a kind of complete grammar, for there are no less than a hundred and twenty different ways of using or placing them, each having a special name according to its function and arrangement.

We often hear of Japanese gardens—so-called—in England, but surely it is unwise, when we are already provided with ample means of horticultural expression of our own, not to speak of what we have learnt from Italy and through Italy from France and Holland, to attempt any kind of reproduction of these far-eastern pleasure grounds, whose whole source of impulse, and whose tradition and sentiment differs so greatly from our own. The nearest that seems permissible is some suggestion of oriental detail of pagoda or bridge with a use of Bamboo and Iris, such as might recall those times of the late 18th century when lacquered ornament of Chinese character was employed on furniture, and in clever hands was found to be well adapted to household decoration. But to assume that we may easily make Japanese gardens in England may leave us defenceless before a just charge of ignorant, or at least somewhat heedless presumption.

The Chinese garden at Biddulph Grange, Cheshire.

The pool mirror.

The Chinese Water Lily (Nelumbium speciosum) in a garden in Japan.

In Prince Horita's garden in Japan.

Bridge and pond in a Japanese garden.

A sacred grove.

A garden of Fukagawa.

In deep shade of Wistaria bloom.

INDEX